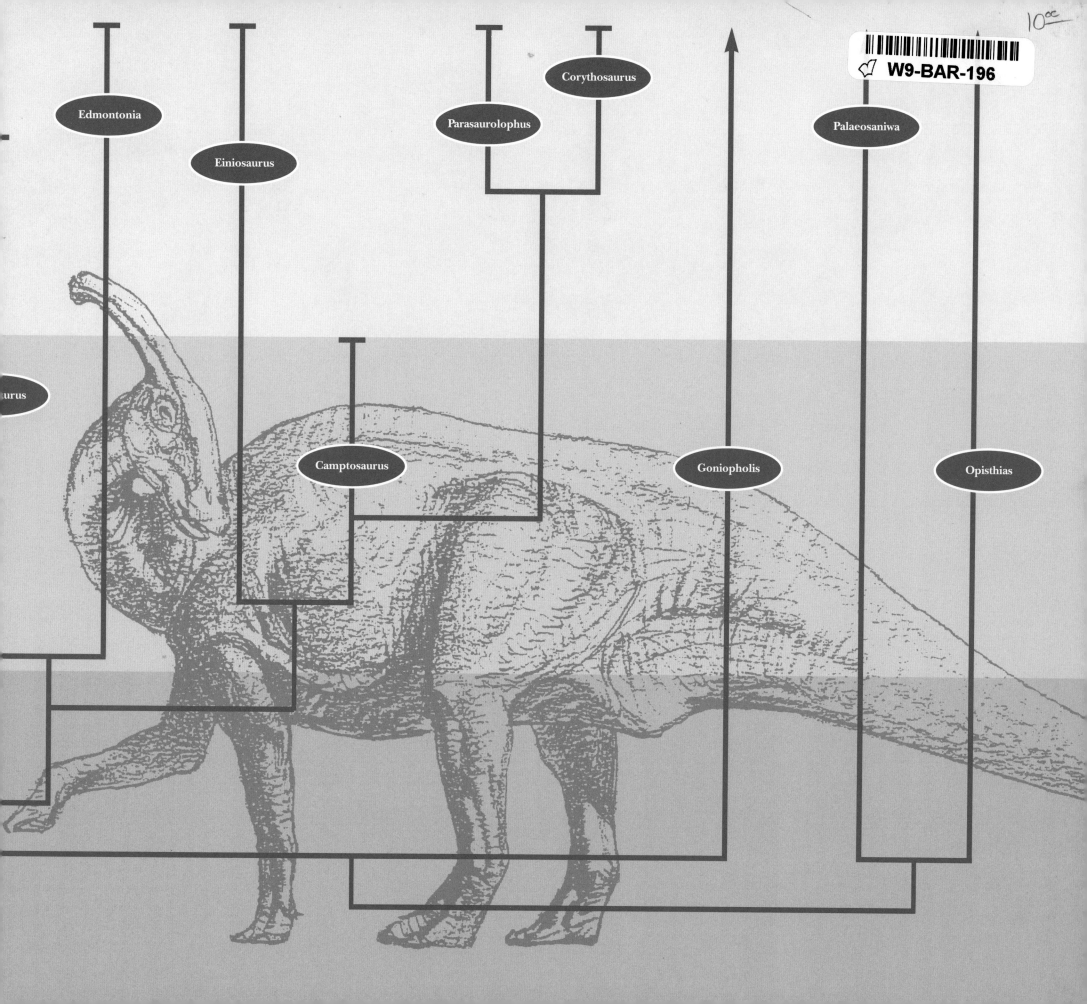

Edmontonia

Einiosaurus

Parasaurolophus

Corythosaurus

Palaeosaniwa

...urus

Camptosaurus

Goniopholis

Opisthias

James Gurney
The World of Dinosaurs

Edmontonia USA 32 / USA 32 *Einiosaurus*

MICHAEL K. BRETT-SURMAN, PH.D.; DR. THOMAS R. HOLTZ, JR.
INTRODUCTION BY JACK HORNER

THE GREENWICH WORKSHOP PRESS

Introduction

Dinosaurs are probably the most recognizable creatures that ever lived. They are the outrageous reality of evolution and extinction! Fantastic, yet preposterous, dinosaurs nourish our imaginations with images of both terror and wonder. For me, dinosaurs are simply astonishing. I am in awe of their skeletons and their footprints and their eggs, and all the other evidence of their existence. And, as far back as I can remember, their mystery was the driving force of my desire to be a dinosaur paleontologist.

When I was young, growing up in Shelby, Montana, I played in the hills behind my parents' house. The hills were made of sediments deposited in an ocean that existed when dinosaurs roamed the world. Like most boys my age, especially in this part of Montana where there was little to do, I picked up and saved all the fossils I could find—clams and snails and ammonites, and even some bones of swimming reptiles called plesiosaurs. I collected so many fossils that I filled a portion of my parents' basement. At age eight, I found my first dinosaur bone, which I still have, and by the time I was in high school, I had found and excavated part of a dinosaur skeleton, which I donated to our local museum.

As much as I loved the discovery part of collecting, I also liked saving and studying. I was intrigued by the mystery of how the animals lived and what the land was like when they were here. I read a lot of books about geology and biology and even about dinosaurs, and then, using my imagination, I would dream about being in the Cretaceous or Jurassic, sneaking up on a dinosaur. Usually a small dinosaur. Sometimes I would take my plastic dinosaur models out into the hills and pretend they were dying. I would cover them with dirt and later uncover them as though working on an excavation.

I wanted to be a paleontologist but never imagined I would actually become one. I loved collecting, but it wasn't just fossils that I gathered and saved and examined and studied. I also saved dinosaur models, and metal junk, and electric gizmos, and ordinary rocks, and coins—and in the wintertime, when the ground was covered with snow, I saved postage stamps, especially ones with pictures of animals and plants. Stamps with dinosaurs were my prize possessions.

When the Postal Service called me and asked if I would consult on the creation of a new dinosaur stamp series to be painted by artist James Gurney, I was thrilled. And I was especially excited when I learned that they wanted to make two scenes, and one of the scenes would depict an area of Montana where I have been doing dinosaur research—the area where I had found and collected thousands of dinosaur skeletons over a period of twenty-five years. It was a scene I had imagined a thousand times, and I had been chosen to help James Gurney, one of the best dinosaur artists of this century, turn it into a scientifically accurate, collectible, yet practical, work of art.

The World of Dinosaurs postage stamps series, upon which this book is based, depicts two scenes from the Mesozoic era in the United States. The Jurassic

• GENTLE GIANTS? •

Camarasaurus was a member of the sauropod dinosaur group which were all herbivores, and are thought to have traveled in herds, protecting their young at the center of the group.

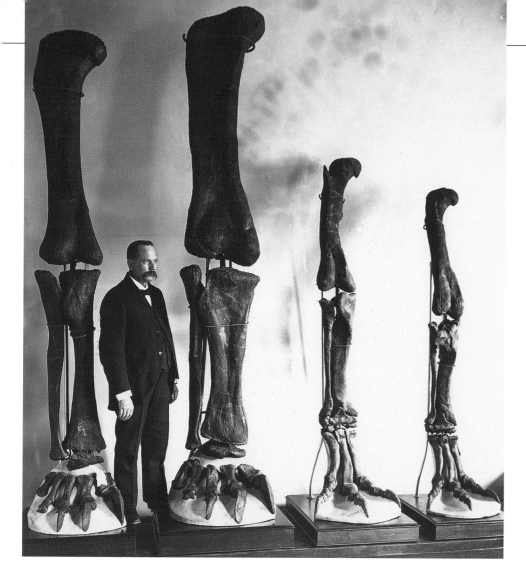

•CIRCA 1899•
(*left*) Adam Hermann developed mounting techniques for treasures from the American Museum of Natural History's early dinosaur-collecting expeditions. He is shown here with the hind limbs of some Jurassic dinosaurs: *Diplodocus, Apatosaurus* and *Allosaurus*.

scene is from Colorado and includes such famous but rare dinosaurs as *Stegosaurus* and *Brachiosaurus*, and several others, and even some lizards and crocodiles. The Cretaceous scene from Montana depicts dinosaurs like *Parasaurolophus* and *Daspletosaurus*, and—my favorite—*Einiosaurus*, a dinosaur that I was lucky enough to have discovered. There is even a monitor lizard in the scene, as well as some furry little mammals. These dinosaurs and other animals lived not only in Montana and Colorado, but all over most of North America. The authors, Dr. Brett-Surman and Dr. Holtz, are both dinosaur paleontologists, and they have put the latest information about dinosaurs in this book so you can learn about new ideas concerning dinosaurs.

Paleontologists are constantly coming up with new ideas and theories about dinosaurs because they are regularly finding new skeletons and new pieces of the dinosaur puzzle. One of the important rules of science is to always be on the lookout for evidence that shows previous ideas to be wrong. This is one of the ways science can be sure that it is objective. In the next few years, some of the things written in this book may be found to have been wrong, and that's fine, because we will have come a little closer to knowing the truth about dinosaurs.

The World of Dinosaurs is exactly what I needed when I was growing up in Shelby, because it not only gives interesting information about dinosaurs and some of the plants and animals that lived with them; it also tells interesting stuff about stamp collecting. There are even pictures of postage stamps from other countries with dinosaurs on them. Looking through this book will give you an idea of how artists work, and how paleontologists work, and how you can learn about both art and paleontology and a world of other things by collecting postage stamps. Now that I'm grown-up, or at least bigger, I still enjoy stamp collecting and discovering dinosaurs. And every once in a while, when I'm really lucky, I find a new dinosaur or a rare postage stamp, and the discovery of either one excites me just as much as it did when I was eight. When you read this book, maybe you, too, will become interested in dinosaurs and stamps, and realize that learning new things about anything is just about the greatest thing a human being can do.

—JACK HORNER
Montana State University
Museum of the Rockies, Bozeman, Montana

Designing Stamps

The United States Postal Service has a rule: a person must be dead for at least ten years before appearing on a postage stamp. Mesozoic dinosaurs have been dead for 65 million years, so they definitely qualify. Over the years, dinosaurs have been used as postage stamp subjects in many other countries. Surprisingly, the United States has featured prehistoric reptiles only twice before in its 150-year history of producing stamps, first in 1970 and again in 1989.

In September of 1995, the United States Postal Service invited me to develop a new set of dinosaur postage stamps. We agreed that the stamps should accurately reflect the new scientific understanding of dinosaurs, something I have also tried to achieve in my Dinotopia books. By presenting these up-to-date dinosaurs in an unusual pictorial format, we hoped to attract more young people and families to postage stamp collecting. The original concept was to include a grouping of four stamps within a larger illustrated scene. The detailed border around the postage stamps themselves would show the natural setting that the dinosaurs inhabited. The design would encourage collectors to keep the pane intact, a point not lost on the agency's marketing department, since a large portion of revenue comes from postage stamps that are purchased but never used.

My first sketches showed four dinosaurs that would have lived during the Late Cretaceous period in North America, including a *Tyrannosaurus rex* and an *Einiosaurus* (with a hooked nose horn), a recently discovered relative of *Triceratops*.

The postage stamp committee liked the ideas in the sketch so much that they wanted to increase the number of stamps to ten. This presented me with a

•FIRST APPROACH WITH FOUR POSTAGE STAMPS•

To the left are a sketch and color study of the original postage stamp proposal. Four dinosaurs are shown together as part of a larger scene extending around the edges. The first sketch shows dinosaurs from the Late Cretaceous period that lived on the land mass which is now North America. The postage stamp committee decided to increase the number of stamps to ten.

•TEN STAMPS IN TWO SCENES•

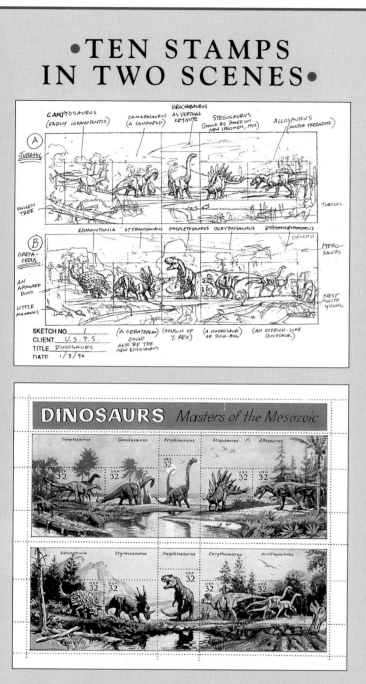

The second sketch and color study is an arrangement of ten postage stamps, five each from the Jurassic and Cretaceous periods. The title of Dinosaurs: Masters of the Mesozoic *was abandoned later when non-dinosaurs were included.*

•POSTAGE STAMP SELECTION CRITERIA•

The stamp committee of the U.S. Postal Service has developed the following criteria for evaluating postage stamp proposals:

- Postage stamp subjects must stand the test of time.
- They should be consistent with public opinion.
- Subjects must have broad national interest.
- U.S. postage stamps and stationery should feature American or American-related subjects.
- Except for U.S. presidents, no person will be honored on a postage stamp or stationery item until ten years after his or her death—usually on a significant birthday.
- U.S. presidents may be honored with a memorial postage stamp on their first birthday after their death.
- Historical events will be considered only on anniversaries in multiples of 50 years.
- Only events and themes of widespread national appeal and significance will be considered.

difficult design problem. Dinosaurs arranged neatly in two rows of five begin to look like chorus-line dancers, with the ones in the back row rearing up unnaturally. So I proposed that the design be divided into two different panoramic scenes, each including a single row of five postage stamps. With two scenes, it became possible to feature well-known dinosaurs from the two great ages of North American dinosaurs, the Jurassic at 150 million years ago and the Cretaceous at 75 million years ago. By turning the center stamp to vertical, I broke up the monot–ony of the row and created a central keynote subject for each scene.

At this point, the project was top secret. The Postal Service offered to supply me with all the necessary research material. They appointed the well-known paleontologist Jack Horner as the official science consultant. Luckily, I had worked with Horner before and had traveled with him to his museum and his fossil sites. To gather even more expert input, I asked permission to contact several other scientists directly, namely Michael Brett-Surman of the Smithsonian Institution, Ken Carpenter of the Denver Museum of Natural History, and Phil Currie of the Royal Tyrrell Museum in Alberta, Canada. (Canada and the U.S. share many of the same dinosaurs.)

These scientists provided lists of contemporaneous dinosaurs to choose from, including old favorites like *Allosaurus* and *Stegosaurus* and lesser-known dinosaurs like *Daspletosaurus*, a cousin of *Tyrannosaurus rex*. They also supplied information about other creatures that would have shared the world with dinosaurs—frogs, turtles, insects, crocodiles, pterosaurs, mammals, and birds—as well as plants: sequoias, cycads, tree ferns, and horsetails.

I wanted to re-create the full texture of this environment in order to make the postage stamps useful as an education tool. Although dinosaurs are often portrayed in a comparatively barren setting, they actually lived in a rich and diverse ecosystem. Many of the plants and animals would have resembled modern forms in Florida today. I wanted the picture to tell a variety of stories, not just of predators looking for a meal, but also of babies hatching from eggs and mammals hiding in trees. To show a fossil in formation, I placed the skull of a *Chasmosaurus* in the mud at the edge of the pond.

Since my specialty is painting realistic images of things that cannot be photographed, I spend many hours studying information that *is* available, both visual and written. In the case of dinosaurs, I start with fossilized bones, footprints, and an occasional impression of skin texture. Drawing a simplified skeleton to scale comes first. Then I flesh out the muscles on tracing paper and add the texture of the skin. Because the pattern of light and shadow can be difficult to invent, I use tabletop models of each dinosaur type, placing the model under a bright light source to study the way wrinkles and scales behave in the

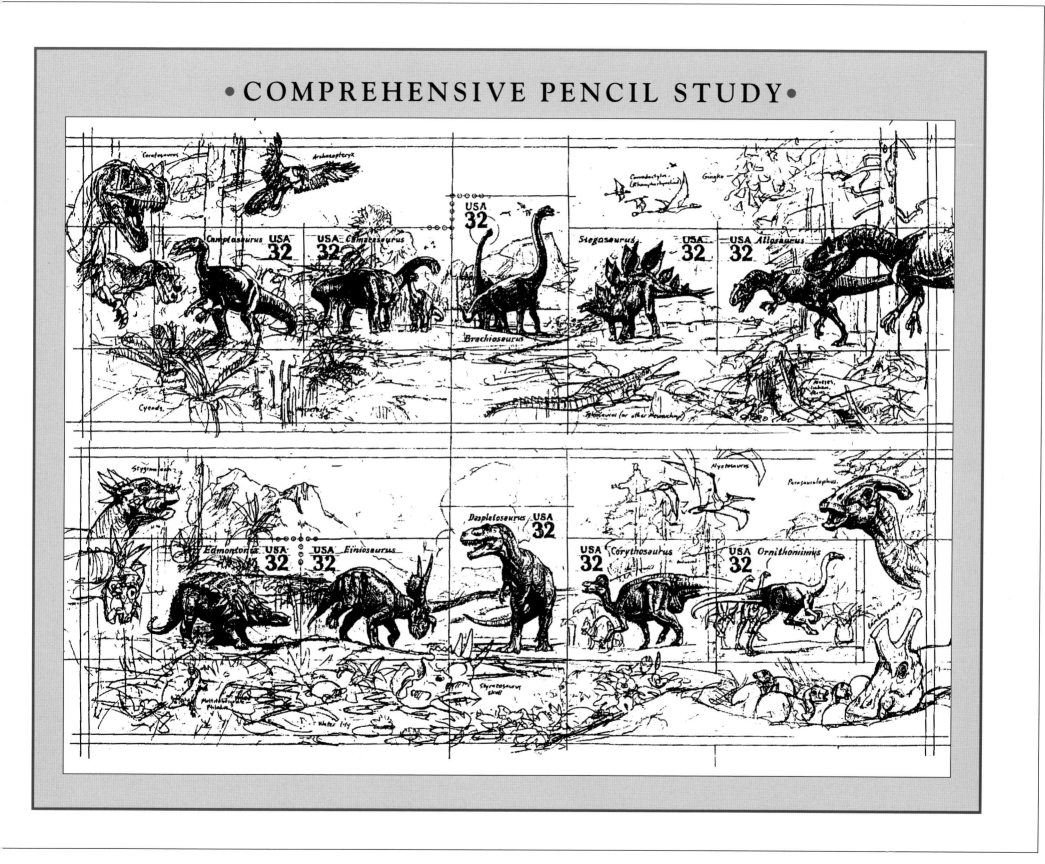

THE WORLD OF DINOSAURS

Ceratosaurus USA 32

Camptosaurus USA 32 · USA 32 *Camarasaurus*

USA 32

Stegosaurus USA 32 · USA 32 *Allosaurus*

Brachiosaurus

Goniopholis

USA 32

Opisthias

USA 32

A scene in Colorado, 150 million years ago

USA 32 *Parasaurolophus*

Daspletosaurus USA 32

Edmontonia USA 32 · USA 32 *Einiosaurus*

USA 32 *Corythosaurus*

USA 32 *Ornithomimus*

.32
x15
$4.80

Palaeosaniwa USA 32

PLATE
POSITION

P11111

© USPS
1996

A scene in Montana, 75 million years ago

light. The colors of the dinosaurs are speculative, of course, because color doesn't fossilize. I like to base the colors on similar patterns from modern animals. *Camptosaurus*, for example, which was a common prey species of the Jurassic, seemed to look best with a coloration similar to that of the Thomson's gazelle, the familiar prey species of East Africa.

For the plants, I traveled to Florida and to the Brooklyn Botanic Garden, taking lots of photographs. I snipped branches from ginkgo trees in my hometown, brought them home, and painted them into the scene just as they appeared. I discovered later that the leaves really had a multilobed shape in the Jurassic, so I had to go back and repaint each leaf, one at a time. I had to paint the ferns outdoors because they wither quickly when cut and brought inside. At one point, a mosquito landed in the wet paint and got stuck. I thought of leaving it there for a little touch of realism, but mosquitoes didn't look quite the same in the Mesozoic, so I had to scrape it off.

The Postal Service enthusiastically approved my final sketches, and while I was finishing the painting, I received a call from the postage stamp committee art director, who suggested that several of the creatures in the margins of the design could be made into additional postage stamps. With a small amount of retouching, five more animals became stamp subjects. Since some of the new subjects were not dinosaurs, the title of the issue was changed from *Dinosaurs: Masters of the Mesozoic* to *The World of Dinosaurs*.

Before long, the paintings were finished and shipped to the printer to be reproduced into more than 200 million postage stamps, enough to span the continent twice if laid end to end.

—JAMES GURNEY

We thought of making a sixteenth postage stamp out of the nest of hatchlings that appears in the bottom right corner of the Jurassic mural. The "USA 32" marking would go in the space in the big egg that hasn't cracked yet. In the end, the Postal Service decided to keep the number of postage stamps at fifteen. While the surrounding art created an exciting and colorful panorama, it was very important that a person could tear up the sheet easily to get at the stamps without being confused about what were postage stamps and what were scraps. Also, we wanted to be sure the margin shapes were big enough to be usable as decorative stickers once the stamps had been torn away.

Ceratosaurus

*C*eratosaurus, "horned reptile," was one of the most distinctive predatory dinosaurs of the Late Jurassic of the American West. At 20 feet (6 meters) long and more than 1,300 pounds (600 kilograms) in weight, it was a medium-sized meat eater in its ecosystem: larger than the smaller carnivorous dinosaurs such as *Ornitholestes*, but smaller than the giant *Allosaurus* and *Torvosaurus*.

Fossils of *Ceratosaurus* have been found in Colorado and Utah, and possible *Ceratosaurus* specimens have been discovered in Wyoming, Oklahoma, and Tanzania, in eastern Africa. Only a few specimens of *Ceratosaurus* are known, as opposed to dozens of skeletons of *Allosaurus*. The best fossil is still the first one found by paleontologists. On display at the Smithsonian Institution's National Museum of Natural History, this skeleton formed the basis of James Gurney's illustration for the postage stamp.

The most obvious feature of *Ceratosaurus* is the "horn" on its nose. Unlike the weapons of the great horned dinosaurs of the Cretaceous, such as *Einiosaurus*, the horn of *Ceratosaurus* was just a narrow crest and was probably simply for display. Perhaps the horns of male and female *Ceratosaurus*, or adult and baby *Ceratosaurus*, were different from each other, as they are in many dinosaurs and other animals. Unfortunately, we have not yet found enough fossils to determine the true nature and purpose of the horn.

Unlike three-fingered *Allosaurus*, *Ceratosaurus* had four fingers on each hand, and they were not well adapted to grasping. However, the jaws and teeth of *Ceratosaurus* were very long and deep, and this dinosaur probably killed its prey by slicing huge chunks off of its victims. Like all meat-eating dinosaurs, *Ceratosaurus* walked only on its hind legs. Along its back, it had a row of small bony bumps—the only known case of "armor" in meat-eating dinosaurs.

Ceratosaurus is one of the best-known representatives of a long-lived group of meat-eating dinosaurs, the Ceratosauria. Other ceratosaurs include long-necked, long-skulled early forms such as *Coelophysis*, *Syntarsus*, and *Dilophosaurus*, and short-necked, deep-skulled *Carnotaurus* and *Abelisaurus*. ●

•HIND LEGS•

Like other meat-eating dinosaurs, *Ceratosaurus* walked on its hind legs, while its hands were free to hold prey.

•CHANGING LOOKS•

Although our knowledge of *Ceratosaurus* has remained the same since its discovery, different artists have restored this dinosaur in different ways. The 1911 restoration (*upper right*) by J. Smit is based on a drawing from 1889. Little attempt has been made to show the curve of the muscles or details of the skin, although the artist did include a *Ceratosaurus* feeding at a corpse. The upper left restoration, done in 1901 by J. M. Gleeson, reflects the artist's knowledge of anatomy and attention to detail. It is one of the most realistic dinosaur reconstructions of its time.

• CERATOSAURUS •
Horned Reptile

Ceratosaurus was a carnivore that walked on its hind legs, much like Tyrannosaurus, *and is identified by its four-fingered hands and a prominent horn on its nose.*

•THE BONES•

Ceratosaurus is best known from this fossil, the almost-complete skeleton on display at the Smithsonian Institution in Washington, D.C. It was the first relatively complete skeleton of a large meat-eating dinosaur ever found, and for the last 100 years it has helped scientists understand the posture and adaptations of Ceratosauria.

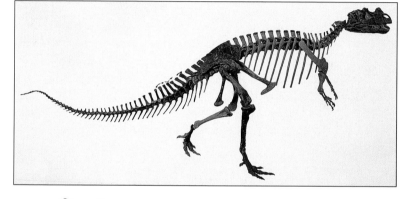

•UNDER IT ALL•

This restoration shows the basic characteristics of *Ceratosaurus:* the deep skull with large teeth, the horn on the nose, and the smaller horns in front of the eyes; the smaller size of the forelimbs, compared to the hind limbs; and the long, deep tail. *Ceratosaurus* is unusual for a meat-eating dinosaur in that there is a small row of bony knobs running down its back.

•ANYONE FOR A SWIM?•

Some people have suggested that the long, deep tail of *Ceratosaurus* helped it swim. While such a tail would have been useful for pushing through the water, no other particular features of the skeleton suggest that it was a swimmer. Of course, almost all animals can swim if they have to.

Camptosaurus

Camptosaurus or "bent lizard," a Late Jurassic dinosaur, was named by Othniel Charles Marsh in 1885, based on material collected in Wyoming. The name "bent lizard" refers to the bent or curved thigh bone of this animal. Most dinosaurs have straight thigh bones, but in this particular dinosaur, the thigh was curved to get the legs farther apart and away from the wide rib cage. The most famous *Camptosaurus* find is at Como Bluff, Albany County, Wyoming. Other sites include Utah, Colorado, Oklahoma, and Great Britain.

Camptosaurus was the first of the ornithopod dinosaurs to become very bottom-heavy. Most of the two-legged ornithopods prior to this time were very light and small. Several features that occur in *Camptosaurus* highlight the transition to larger sizes. There are more vertebrae attached to the pelvis; the legs are thicker than in earlier ornithopods, and the area for muscle attachment for the hind legs is much larger. Some specimens of *Camptosaurus* were about 22 feet (7 meters) long and weighed more than a ton. The arms were much smaller than the legs; therefore, this dinosaur spent most of its time walking on two legs. Although *Camptosaurus* was smaller, and probably slower, than the preda-

tors at this time (such as *Ceratosaurus* and *Allosaurus*), its powerful legs and wide hips may have made it more maneuverable during a chase.

Several species have been named *Camptosaurus,* but paleontologist Peter Galton has shown that the changes seen between the skeletons are due to differences in the age of the animals; hence most paleontologists recognize only one species in North America today—*Camptosaurus dispar.*

The closest relatives of *Camptosaurus* are the dryosaurs, which also lived in the same place and time. Later descendants include *Iguanodon* (Early Cretaceous) and, ultimately, the hadrosaurs in the Late Cretaceous. The models James Gurney used to paint this postage stamp are the two specimens of *Camptosaurus* mounted for exhibit in the National Museum of Natural History at the Smithsonian Institution. The smaller specimen was probably under three years old. ●

•CAMPTOSAURUS•
Bent Lizard

Ranging from 11 to 23 feet long, Campto-saurus was an herbivore of the Late Jurassic and possibly Early Cretaceous periods. Fossils are found predominantly in western North America and Great Britian.

•FAMILY REUNION•

Collectively called iguanodontids, this group represents the closest relatives of *Campto-saurus*, including *Iguanodon* and the sail-backed *Ouranosaurus*.

•ATTACK FROM BEHIND•

This exhibit tells the story of *Allosaurus* attacking *Camptosaurus*. Although *Allosaurus* was faster, *Camptosaurus* was more maneuverable because it had wider hips and relatively thicker legs and feet.

•TIGHT-LIPPED!•

Camptosaurus was one of the first ornithopods to have two rows of teeth. Each tooth was thick, with a large central ridge that went from crown to base. The teeth were ever-growing, and they pushed out older, worn teeth from below. In life, *Camptosaurus* may have used up hundreds of teeth. Humans have a total of only 44.

Camarasaurus

Another contemporary of *Camptosaurus* was the much larger sauropod *Camarasaurus*, "chambered lizard." This herbivore was named by Edward Drinker Cope in 1877. The name refers to the many hollow chambers and excavation on the sides of the backbones (vertebrae). Although *Camarasaurus* is one of the most common fossils in the famous Morrison Formation (Late Jurassic) of the Rocky Mountain states, it never achieved the fame of the other sauropods from the same time and place, such as *Apatosaurus* and *Diplodocus*. *Camarasaurus* is also found in Portugal and Zimbabwe.

The largest herbivores in the Jurassic period were sauropods. *Camarasaurus* was smaller than most other sauropods, but it was very heavily built, with wide, heavy legs, a relatively shorter neck, and a very boxlike skull. The teeth were unique in that they looked like spoons! They had long, thick roots, and enamel covered the parts above the gum line. In order to make room for the long-rooted teeth, the nose was pushed backward to a position above and between the eyes. Such a heavily muscled head and thick teeth were adapted for feeding on hard, fibrous plants. *Camarasaurus* did not cut or nip off plants and chew them the way modern mammals do. Instead, it ripped plant material off bushes and trees and then swallowed it whole. Sauropods did not chew food —their mouths and teeth were not designed like mammals! After swallowing the plant material, the powerful stomach, probably with the help of stomach stones, did the grinding.

The closest relatives of *Camarasaurus* were brachiosaurs and titanosaurs. The first group was common in the Jurassic, and the second group were the most numerous sauropods of the Cretaceous. In 1997, paleontologists Jeff Wilson and Paul Sereno named these three groups of sauropods the Macronaria, which means "big nose."

The most famous specimen, and the basis for this postage stamp, is the juvenile (teenager) on display in the Carnegie Museum of Natural History in Pittsburgh, Pennsylvania. This is one of the most complete dinosaur skeletons ever found! ●

•CAMARASAURUS•
Chambered Lizard

Camarasaurus, *one of the most abundant sauropods, was closely related to the brachiosaurs and titanosaurs, although it was smaller than these two groups. It was common in Wyoming, Colorado, and Utah.*

•TEETH AND DIET•
Thick teeth with long roots allowed *Camarasaurus* to feed on hard-fiber plants, like bushes and trees, that others found difficult to strip.

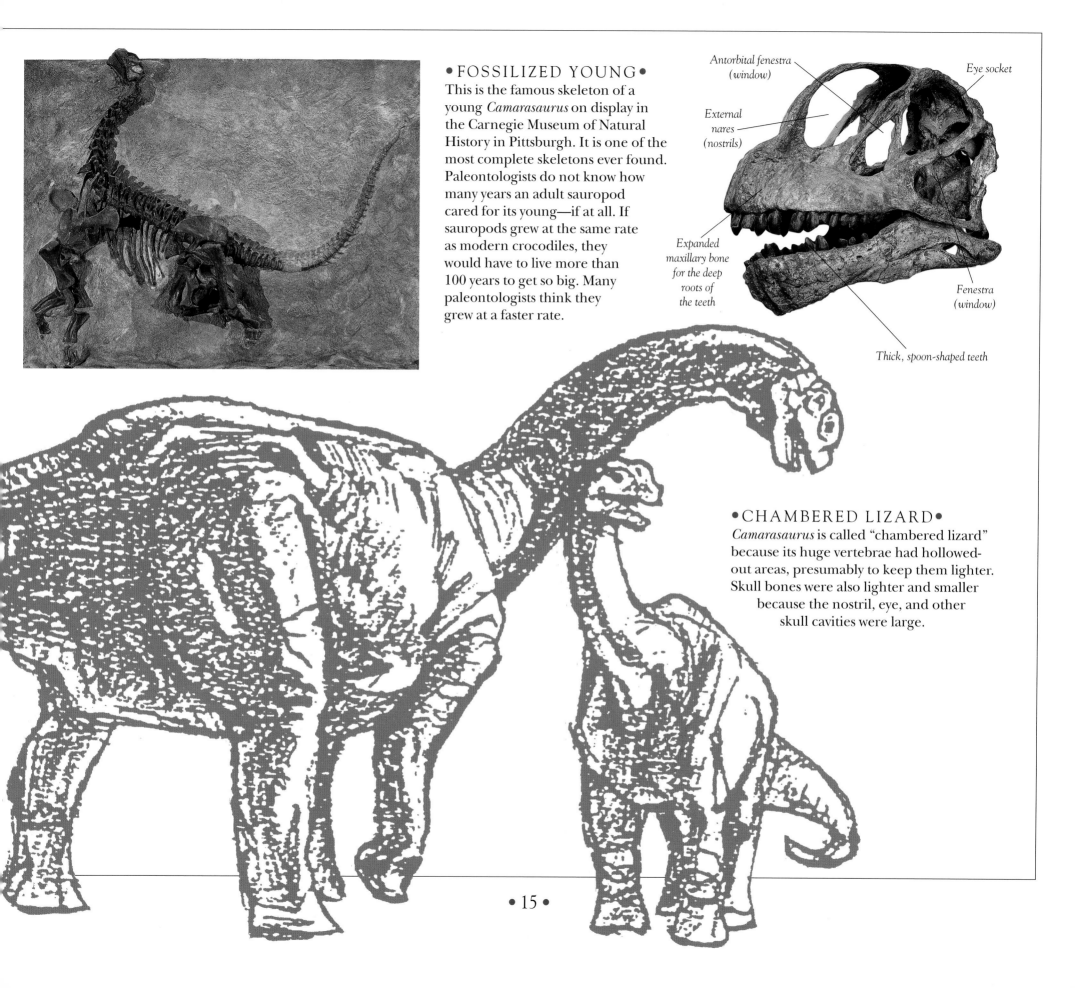

•FOSSILIZED YOUNG•

This is the famous skeleton of a young *Camarasaurus* on display in the Carnegie Museum of Natural History in Pittsburgh. It is one of the most complete skeletons ever found. Paleontologists do not know how many years an adult sauropod cared for its young—if at all. If sauropods grew at the same rate as modern crocodiles, they would have to live more than 100 years to get so big. Many paleontologists think they grew at a faster rate.

Antorbital fenestra (window)

Eye socket

External nares (nostrils)

Expanded maxillary bone for the deep roots of the teeth

Fenestra (window)

Thick, spoon-shaped teeth

•CHAMBERED LIZARD•

Camarasaurus is called "chambered lizard" because its huge vertebrae had hollowed-out areas, presumably to keep them lighter. Skull bones were also lighter and smaller because the nostril, eye, and other skull cavities were large.

Brachiosaurus

B*rachiosaurus*, "arm lizard," was named in 1903 by Elmer Riggs of the Field Columbian Museum, now the Field Museum of Natural History, in Chicago, Illinios. It was named "arm lizard" because at the time it was found, it was the only dinosaur with arms longer than the hind legs. Although the original specimen was found in Colorado, other specimens have come from Europe and East Africa. During the Late Jurassic, it would have been possible to walk from Colorado to Africa because the continents had not yet separated into their present positions.

A human standing next to *Brachiosaurus* would only come up to the elbow. The obvious question is "Why did they get so big?" The answer is that the adults would have had exclusive access to plants high up in the trees. They were not in competition for food with other sauropods, or even with their own young. Large size in itself was also the best defense. *Allosaurus* and *Ceratosaurus* would not attack a full-grown adult. *Brachiosaurus* is one of the few animals in earth history where the front limbs are longer than the hind limbs. Can you name any others? Their height is quite impressive when you consider that this dinosaur's head was about 50 feet off the ground. If you want to know what this is like, go to a window on the fifth floor of a building and look down the side of the building. Pretend your shoes are at the bottom and that this is how you will forever view the world, looking down from this height.

The model for this postage stamp was the mounted skeleton on display in Chicago. It is partly cast from a specimen in the Humboldt Museum in Germany. New studies have shown that the family Brachiosauridae is most closely related to the Cretaceous sauropod family, the Titanosauridae. ●

• BRACHIOSAURUS •
Arm Lizard

A giant plant eater of the Jurassic period, Brachiosaurus *was one of the tallest known land animals of all time. The neck alone was nearly 30 feet long, and specimens weighed as much as 80 tons. Scientists study this dinosaur to see how a skeleton can be designed to withstand such great weight and still be mobile.*

• BONES •
This fine skeletal restoration is based on several skeletons in various museums. Note that the neck is longer than the tail and that the front limbs are longer than the hind limbs. The flesh restoration (*right*) shows how the teeth and jaws make up the entire front half of the head. The gape of the mouth could have been wider than the entire skull of *Allosaurus*.

Footprints

•THE HEAD BONE'S CONNECTED...•

Brachiosaurus had a skull that was mostly filled with air space! By combining the engineering concept of using bone for struts and braces, the skull is light, yet very strong. It would be another 150 million years before humans rediscovered this principle.

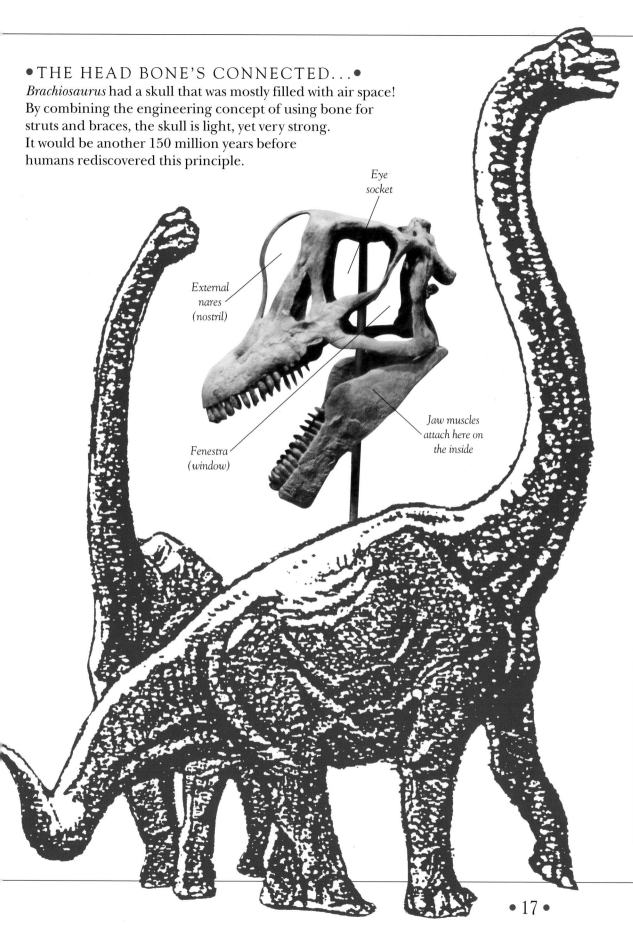

Eye socket

External nares (nostril)

Fenestra (window)

Jaw muscles attach here on the inside

•A FINE SPECIMEN•

There is only one mounted skeleton of *Brachiosaurus* on display in the western hemisphere—and it is in the Field Museum of Natural History in Chicago. The one shown below is on display at the Humboldt Museum in Berlin, Germany. Notice how the huge forelimbs are much taller than the hind legs. This allowed the head and mouth to be that much higher, the better to eat off the treetops. No complete skeleton, with skull, has ever been found of this giant. If it were discovered, it would take more than four years to dig it up and prepare it for exhibit.

•17•

Goniopholis

N ot all the creatures living in the Late Jurassic of the American West were dinosaurs. In the shadow of the dinosaurs lived animals we would find familiar today: insects, frogs, and salamanders; primitive mammals; turtles and tortoises; lizards and lizard relatives (such as *Opisthias*); and crocodilians. *Goniopholis*, "angled scutes," is a typical Jurassic crocodilian.

First named from Early Cretaceous fossils from Great Britain, *Goniopholis*, or species closely related to it, is known from teeth and fragments of skeletons from the Morrison Formation of the American West. Similar specimens are found in many Late Jurassic and Early Cretaceous fossils worldwide.

From its outward appearance, *Goniopholis* would not have looked dramatically different from a small modern crocodile—a South American caiman or a young Nile crocodile, for example. In fact, it probably lived and behaved in a very similar fashion to modern crocodiles, spending most of its life floating in rivers and ponds or sunning on the banks, and occasionally hiding in the water, waiting for a fish or small animal, such as a baby dinosaur, to come by so it could lunge forth and grab it. Some details of the skull and the teeth, which, like those of meat-eating dinosaurs, had a row of tiny serrations down the front and back, show that *Goniopholis* was more primitive than modern crocodiles and alligators.

Although *Goniopholis* itself looked very much like a modern Nile crocodile, other crocodilians from the age of dinosaurs were very different from modern forms. The first crocodilians—from around 235 million years ago, the same age as the first dinosaurs and first mammals—were small, long-legged running animals, not the swimming creatures we think of today. On the other hand, some Jurassic crocodiles were so specialized for life at sea that their arms and legs evolved into flippers and their tails developed fishlike fins. Toward the end of the Cretaceous period, some crocodilians became huge: *Deinosuchus* was perhaps 45–50 feet (12–15 meters) long! It could have easily preyed on most dinosaurs that came to its ponds and rivers, although recent evidence suggests that the preferred food of this giant crocodile was huge turtles. ●

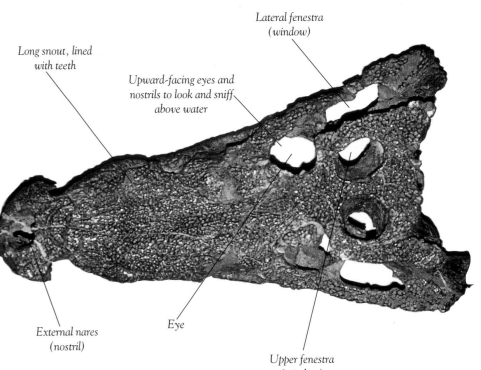

Long snout, lined with teeth

Lateral fenestra (window)

Upward-facing eyes and nostrils to look and sniff above water

External nares (nostril)

Eye

Upper fenestra (window)

•GONIOPHOLIS•
In general appearance and behavior, *Goniopholis* was very similar to the crocodiles of today.

•ALLIGATORS AND CROCODILES•

Alligators—including the South American caimans—and crocodiles are the two major types of modern crocodilians. The third is the long-snouted gharial or gavial of India. Alligators and crocodiles eat fish, turtles, each other, and the occasional land mammal, such as this unlucky antelope. Alligators and crocodiles can lie in wait for long periods of time, then strike very quickly to seize their victim. *Goniopholis* probably killed small dinosaurs in just this fashion.

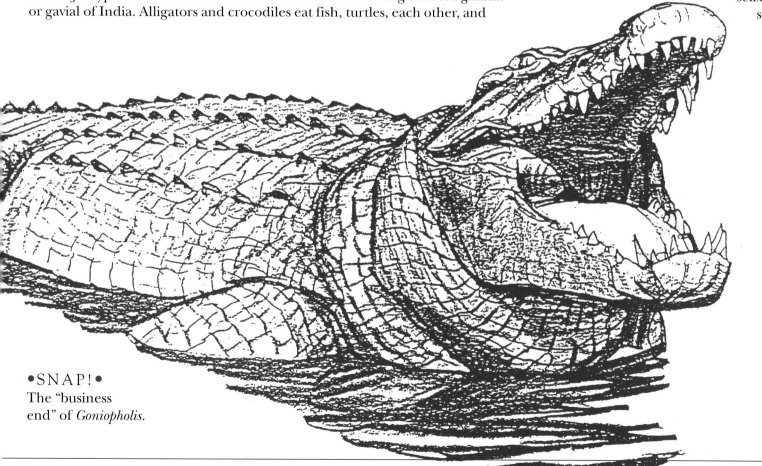

•GONIOPHOLIS•
Angled Scutes

A crocodile of the Late Jurassic period, Goniopholis *is peculiar for its interlocking armored scales. It became extinct during the Mesozoic era, but it was remarkably similar to today's crocodiles.*

•SNAP!•
The "business end" of *Goniopholis*.

Stegosaurus

Stegosaurus or "roof lizard," a Late Jurassic plated dinosaur, was named in 1877 by Othniel Charles Marsh of Yale University. Its name refers to the series of plates that runs down the back of the animal. The two most famous sites for specimens of *Stegosaurus* are Como Bluff, Wyoming, and Garden Park, near Canyon City, Colorado. The two most complete specimens in the world came from Garden Park, and a baby *Stegosaurus* was found at Dinosaur National Monument in Utah.

Stegosaurus had two famous features: the plates and the tail spikes. The plates served many functions. They made the dinosaur look a lot bigger than it would without them, and they were large enough to help in species recognition from a distance. In the mid-1970s, James Farlow showed that the plates could also act as a form of temperature control. When *Stegosaurus* stood in the sun, the plates would absorb heat and help warm the animal. In the shade, the plates would cool quickly. The tail spikes used to be pictured as pointing up and slightly to the side. A new specimen, found in 1990 by Ken Carpenter and Bryan Small of the Denver Museum of Natural History, showed that the spikes actually pointed sideways.

The stegosaurs as a group were one of the two rarest groups of dinosaurs, the other being pachycephalosaurs. There are only about a dozen Stegosaurid species known in the entire world, and only two from the Late Jurassic have been found in Wyoming. Earlier stegosaurs had spikes, with plates appearing later. These bones were not like "regular" bones in the body. The plates and spikes grew out of the skin! We know from fossils that stegosaurs were slow-moving herbivores with very small brains, considering their body size.

The closest relatives of *Stegosaurus* are other members of the

• STEGOSAURUS •
Roof Lizard

This is the first postage stamp of Stegosaurus to show the latest scientific information about its appearance. Note how the spikes point out to the sides, and how short the tail is compared to that of the sauropods.

family Stegosauridae from Europe, and many forms in China. The closest relatives of the stegosaur family are the ankylosaurs, which replaced stegosaurs.

The models for this postage stamp are the *Stegosaurus* on display at the Smithsonian Institution's National Museum of Natural History, and the more complete specimen now at Garden Park, Colorado. The former specimen is on exhibit as it was found in the field. The latter specimen has been fully restored, and a cast is mounted on display at the Denver Museum of Natural History. ●

• BIRD'S-EYE VIEW •
This is the view that a pterosaur might have had of *Stegosaurus*. Even though this dinosaur was the size of a rhinocerous, its skull was no bigger than that of a large dog.

•TAIL SPIKE AND PLATE•

Stegosauria had many different combinations of spikes and plates. *Dacentrurus* had only spikes, whereas *Huayangosaurus*, a Middle Jurassic genus found in China, had both spikes and plates down its back. All stegosaurs' tails had large spikes. A stegosaurid spike could be as long as 4 feet (1.2 meters). The spiked tail was probably for defense in battle and may also have been used as a display of superiority.

Plates were arranged in a single row alternating either to the right or left

The bases were thick and deeply embedded in the skin

In life, the spike was probably covered with hard, hornlike material

Base of the spike

• THE FIRST SPECIMEN •

(below) This is the famous original specimen of *Stegosaurus stenops* at the Smithsonian Institution in Washington, D.C., where it is on exhibit. It is displayed as it was found in the field, showing how the back part of the specimen was scattered before final burial.

•DEFENSE!•

Two of the most complete skeletons found show a network of hundreds of small bony studs protecting the throat area.

Allosaurus

Of all the predators of the Late Jurassic of the American West, *Allosaurus,* "different lizard," is the most famous and the best understood. Named by Othniel Charles Marsh in 1877, the first fragmentary fossil of this theropod dinosaur was collected at the famous Garden Park quarry in Fremont County, Colorado. Since then, many dozens of skeletons and thousands of isolated bones and teeth of *Allosaurus* have been collected across the American West, in Colorado, Montana, New Mexico, Oklahoma, Wyoming, Utah, and South Dakota. At the Cleveland-Lloyd Dinosaur Quarry of Utah, bones of at least 44 different *Allosaurus* individuals, ranging from small babies to huge adults, were found together. Whether this represents the catastrophic kill of a huge *Allosaurus* pack or simply the accumulation of one or two dying dinosaurs at a time over a long span is not yet known. Possible *Allosaurus* fossils have been found in Tanzania, eastern Africa, and Australia, but these may be the bones of different, but closely related, allosaurs.

Allosaurus was typically around 30 feet (10 meters) long and 2 tons in weight, although some individuals may have reached 40 feet (13 meters) and 5 tons. Like most meat-eating dinosaurs, *Allosaurus* had jaws lined with long, sharp teeth that had small serrations, like on a steak knife, running down the front and back. The skull of *Allosaurus* was somewhat flexible, and some paleontologists think this might have allowed the dinosaur to swallow very large chunks of meat or to withstand the stress of the victim wriggling in its jaws. The three-fingered hands of *Allosaurus* were tipped with long, curved claws shaped like the talons of eagles. Backed by strong arm muscles, these claws were well adapted to grasping a struggling plant eater. The claws of the three main toes were not as strongly curved but may have helped hold the prey while the dinosaur fed. Like all advanced meat-eating dinosaurs, *Allosaurus* had a wishbone.

The basic allosaur body design endured a very long time. The smaller *Cryo–lophosaurus* was present in the Early Jurassic, while *Acrocanthosaurus* and *Neovenator* were found in the Early Cretaceous. Two giant Mid-Cretaceous allosaurs, enormous *Giganotosaurus* and *Carcharodontosaurus,* are the largest predatory dinosaurs known. However, these huge forms died out long before the end of the Mesozoic and were replaced by the somewhat smaller but more sophisticated tyrannosaurids, such as *Daspletosaurus,* in North America and Asia, and advanced ceratosaurs in Europe and the southern continents. ●

•ALLOSAURUS•
A pair of the predatory dinosaurs, stalking the world of the Late Jurassic in search of meat.

• SKELETON •

This is one of the most complete skeletons of *Allosaurus* ever found. The specimen at right is from an adolescent, found in Wyoming. Skeletons of *Allosaurus* are found all across the American West. From the different skeletons, paleontologists can try to determine how *Allosaurus* changed as it grew up, how males and females differed in size and appearance, and even if more than one species of *Allosaurus* lived at the same time.

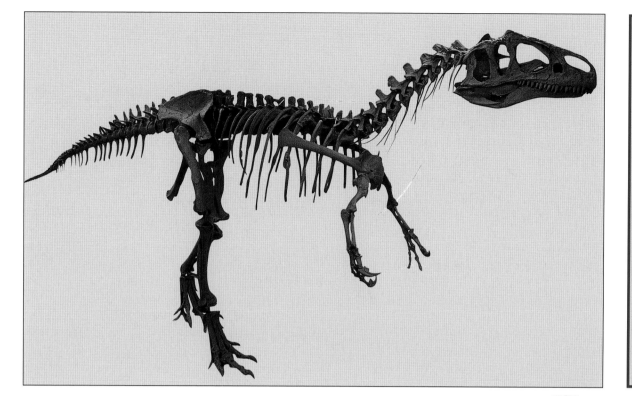

• ALLOSAURUS •
Different Lizard

This huge, 4-ton carnivore was fast, powerful, and armed with a sharp claw on each of its fingers. A group of 44 of these fearsome predators was found in one site in Utah.

• BALANCE •

The long tail of *Allosaurus* balanced the strong front end, useful while the dinosaur was running, turning, or even just scratching an itch.

• STALKING •

This restoration of *Allosaurus* is based on the specimen at the Smithsonian Institution and is shown as if it were slowly stalking a victim.

Opisthias

Although many creatures have changed greatly since the Late Jurassic, some of the forms present at that time survive in a very similar form today. Sometimes called "living fossils," these forms may have been adapted to a life habit that has remained relatively constant over a long period of time. The tuatara, *Sphenodon punctatus*, is often considered such a living fossil. Found today only on the islands of New Zealand, the tuatara is the last surviving member of a once worldwide and diverse group of reptiles, the sphenodontians. Although they resemble lizards, sphenodontians are not true lizards, but rather a related group of reptiles with specialized teeth and jaws. The modern tuatara grows to about 2 feet (61 centimeters) in length and lives on a diet of insects, worms, and other small animals. Many of the fossil sphenodontians were about the same size and had similar diets, although a few may have eaten plants.

Sphenodontians first appeared in the Middle Triassic, before the rise of the dinosaurs. Among the sphenodontians found in the Late Jurassic of the American West is *Opisthias*. First named and described by Charles Whitney Gilmore in 1910, based on material from Wyoming, *Opisthias* is known only from fragmentary fossils. However, there is enough material to indicate that this early tuatara was fairly similar to the modern *Sphenodon* and to other Jurassic sphenodontians such as *Clevosaurus* and *Homoeosaurus*. James Gurney's illustration on the postage stamp shows a form very similar to the modern tuatara. Because of the skeletal similarity of most fossil sphenodontians to the tuatara, it is believed that the ecology of the extinct forms was much the same as that of the New Zealand *Sphenodon*.

Not all Mesozoic sphenodontians were as similar to the modern form. During the Jurassic, one branch of this family evolved into swimming forms. These marine sphenodontians, or pleurosaurs, were long-bodied fish eaters. Their long snouts looked very different in shape from the short, blunt skulls of other sphenodontians, but the details of their bones show that they originated from the typical land-living forms. Sphenodontians thus serve as important evidence of how the anatomy of animals evolves in response to a new or changing environment. ●

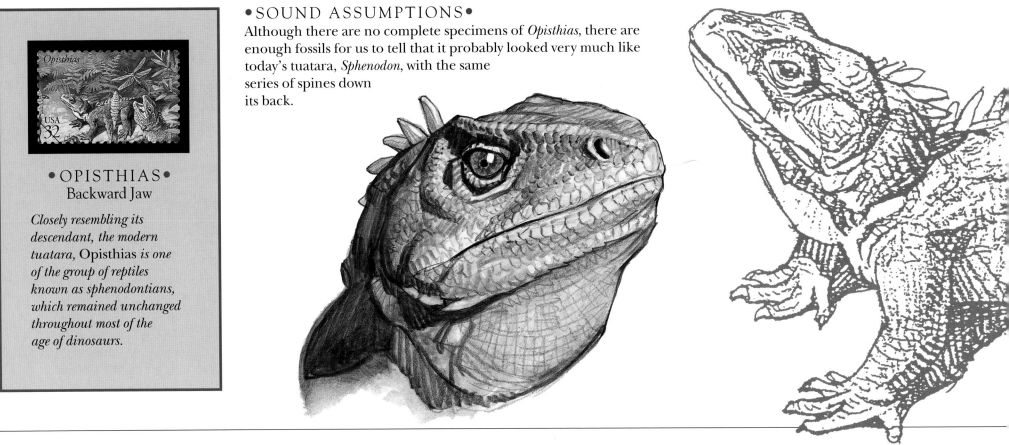

•OPISTHIAS•
Backward Jaw

Closely resembling its descendant, the modern tuatara, Opisthias *is one of the group of reptiles known as sphenodontians, which remained unchanged throughout most of the age of dinosaurs.*

•SOUND ASSUMPTIONS•
Although there are no complete specimens of *Opisthias*, there are enough fossils for us to tell that it probably looked very much like today's tuatara, *Sphenodon*, with the same series of spines down its back.

Opisthias

USA 32

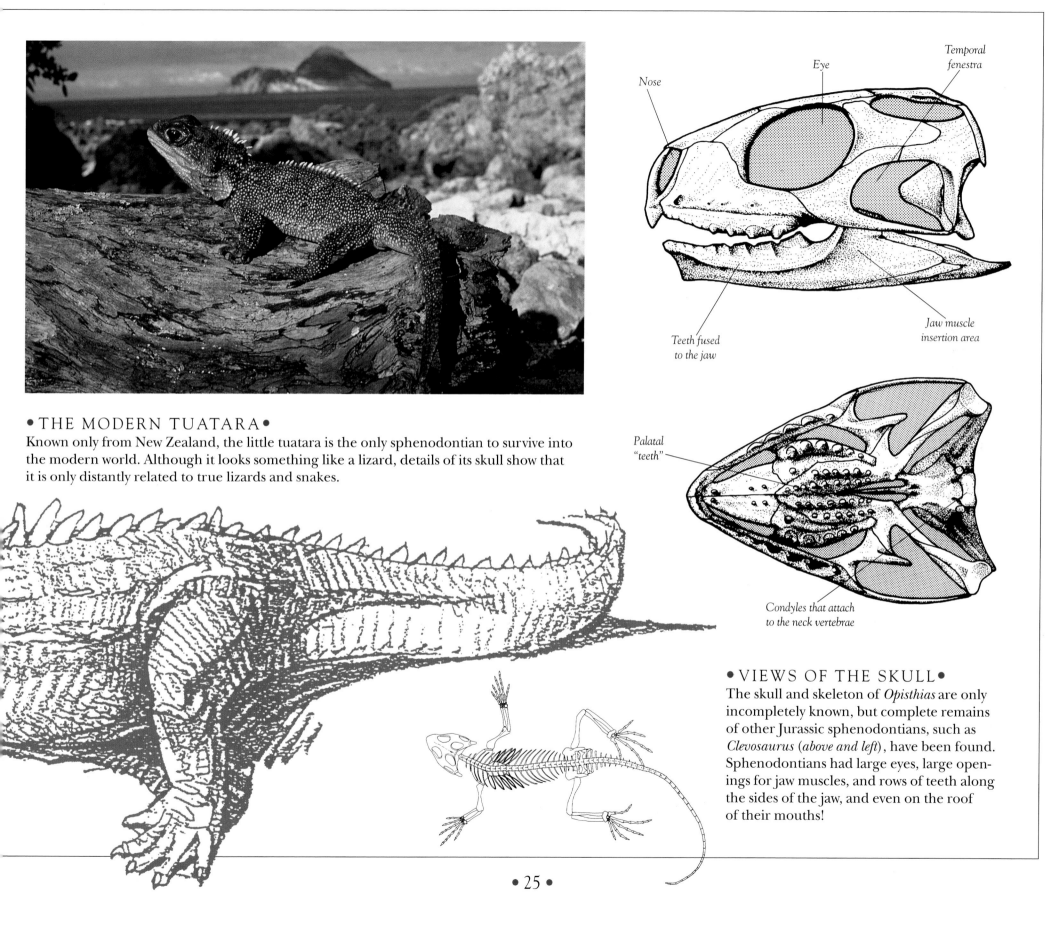

Nose

Eye

Temporal fenestra

Teeth fused to the jaw

Jaw muscle insertion area

Palatal "teeth"

Condyles that attach to the neck vertebrae

• THE MODERN TUATARA •

Known only from New Zealand, the little tuatara is the only sphenodontian to survive into the modern world. Although it looks something like a lizard, details of its skull show that it is only distantly related to true lizards and snakes.

• VIEWS OF THE SKULL •

The skull and skeleton of *Opisthias* are only incompletely known, but complete remains of other Jurassic sphenodontians, such as *Clevosaurus* (*above and left*), have been found. Sphenodontians had large eyes, large openings for jaw muscles, and rows of teeth along the sides of the jaw, and even on the roof of their mouths!

What Are Dinosaurs?

Although some people call any large prehistoric animal a "dinosaur," this term actually applies to a specific group of animals. None of the great sea reptiles were dinosaurs, nor was fin-backed *Dimetrodon*, which was not even a true reptile, but an ancestor of the mammals. The flying pterosaurs, including the pterodactyls, were not dinosaurs, but they were close relatives.

Sir Richard Owen named the Dinosauria, "fearfully great lizards" (more often incorrectly translated as "terrible lizards"), in 1842. Owen recognized that three British fossil reptiles—*Megalosaurus*, *Iguanodon*, and *Hylaeosaurus*—differed from all other forms in having upright limbs (not sprawling, as in lizards or crocodilians), three or more hip vertebrae (not just two), and specialized ribs.

In many ways, Owen thought, the dinosaurs may have been more like mammals or birds than like typical reptiles, and he even suggested that they were warm-blooded, as some paleontologists believe today. Many kinds of dinosaurs have been found since Owen's day, showing that they were a very diverse group of animals. Paleontologists now recognize dinosaurs as that group of animals that descended from the most recent common ancestor of *Megalosaurus* and *Iguanodon*.

The first dinosaurs appeared in the Late Triassic period, around 235 million years ago, at the same time as the first mammals, first crocodiles, and first turtles. *Iguanodon* and all dinosaurs more closely related to it than to *Megalosaurus* are called the Ornithischia, or "bird-hipped." Ornithischians had backward-pointing hip bones, muscular cheeks (like mammals), and a special extra bone at the end of their lower jaw. There were three main groups of ornithischians. The Thyreophora, "shield bearers," were the armored dinosaurs: stegosaurians, ankylosaurians, and their ancestors. The Ornithopoda, "bird feet," lacked armor but had more sophisticated teeth and jaws. Early ornithopods were all two-legged runners, but later and larger forms, such as the duckbills, probably spent much of their life walking on all fours. The Marginocephalia, "ridge heads," are the dome-headed and the horned dinosaurs, groups that used their specialized skulls in display or combat among their own species and against predators.

Megalosaurus and all dinosaurs more closely related to it than to *Iguanodon* form the Saurischia, or "lizard-hipped." There were two main divisions of the saurischians. The long-necked plant eaters form the Sauropodomorpha, "lizard foot forms." The earlier "prosauropods" could walk both on two legs and on all fours, but the later Sauropoda, "lizard feet," such as *Camarasaurus* and *Brachiosaurus*, were so enormous that they could walk only on all fours. The Theropoda, "beast feet," however, were all two-legged forms. Most of the theropods, such as *Ceratosaurus*, *Allosaurus*, *Daspletosaurus*, and *Velociraptor*, were meat eaters, but others, such as *Ornithomimus*, ate some plants. The skeletal anatomy of dinosaurs and primitive birds demonstrates that birds evolved from small theropods closely related to *Velociraptor*. Under the modern system of classification, birds are theropod saurischian dinosaurs. Therefore, the Dinosauria are not extinct, but survive around the world to modern times!

All the other groups of dinosaurs died out at the end of the Cretaceous period, 65 million years ago. ●

• JURASSIC AND CRETACEOUS WHO'S WHO •

(left) Stegoceras, a pachycephalosaur or "dome-headed" dinosaur. These bipedal plant eaters of the Cretaceous were closely related to the horned dinosaurs like *Triceratops* and *Einiosaurus*. *(top right) Archaeopteryx*, the oldest known flying bird. The skeleton of this Jurassic period creature demonstrates that birds evolved from small, carnivorous theropod dinosaurs. *(bottom right) Hesperornis*, a flightless diving bird of the Cretaceous period. During the Cretaceous, birds diversified into many different forms, including fliers, runners, and swimmers. *(far right) Lambeosaurus*, a crested duckbill dinosaur from the Cretaceous and a close relative of *Corythosaurus*.

Dinosaur Hot Spots

Did you know that about 300 million years ago, *all* of Earth's continents were together and formed one huge continent? Scientists began to understand this when they found fossils of a small reptile called *Mesosaurus* only on Brazil's east coast and Africa's west coast. Fossils of large leafy plants like *Glossopteris* were found only in today's Southern Hemisphere, in places as far away from each other as South America, South Africa, and even Australia. These clues indicated to scientists that the continents had been connected and had moved around and collided again more than once in Earth's history. We now refer to that combined land mass as Pangaea.

The breakup of Pangaea into today's continents happened very slowly during the Mesozoic. At 70 million years ago, there was a large, shallow sea that separated the east and west parts of the United States. In fact, for most of the Mesozoic era, this seaway, called an *epeiric sea*, covered what is now the Great Plains. This sea blocked animal migration from east to west on land, so the western half of the United States actually had closer ties to Asia across Alaska and into China and Siberia. This allowed a common *fauna* (animal life) to develop. Migration was frequent from Asia into western North America. Similarly, eastern North America and Europe shared a common fauna.

A flat, coastal plain stretched out on both sides of the sea, and it ended on the west side with the newly formed Rocky Mountains. The climate was wet, warm, and lush, similar to Louisiana today. Rivers and flooding dropped sediment along the edge of the sea, making the area an ideal place for tracks and bones to become fossilized over time. Tracks left here hardened and then were covered under many more layers of rock.

There are a few reasons why dinosaur fossils are more frequently found in the greater Rocky Mountain region than in other parts of the country. Out West, the sedimentary terrestrial rocks from the Mesozoic era are exposed on the surface in arid areas, with little plant cover to hide the bones as they erode out of the rock. There are also fewer people. (It is hard to see fossils when they are buried under a shopping mall!) The fossil areas in the Rocky Mountain states cover most of the Mesozoic era, with a few exceptions such as the Middle Jurassic period. The fossil localities on the East Coast are much rarer and represent only three slices of time—about 210 million years ago, 110 million years ago, and 75 to 65 million years ago. ●

1939, Glen Rose, Texas. Fossil dinosaur footprints were sold by locals as rock garden ornaments before scientists took notice of their importance.

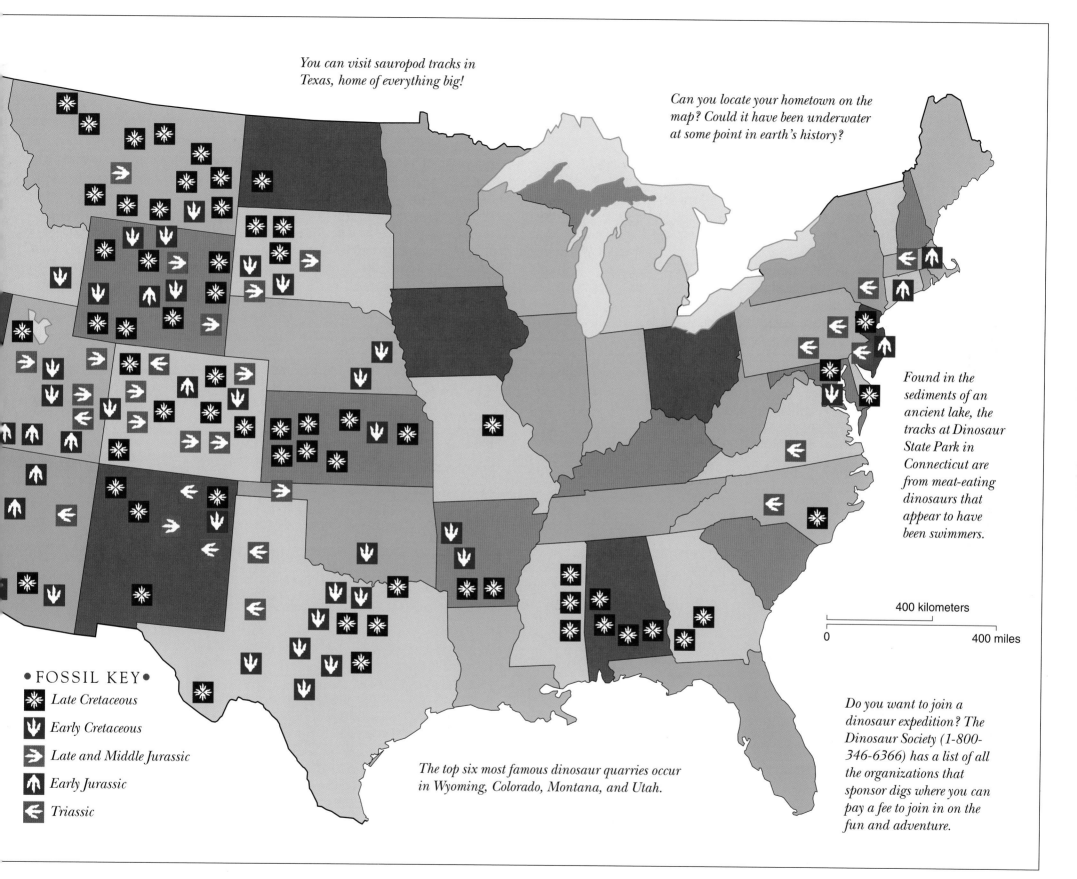

You can visit sauropod tracks in Texas, home of everything big!

Can you locate your hometown on the map? Could it have been underwater at some point in earth's history?

Found in the sediments of an ancient lake, the tracks at Dinosaur State Park in Connecticut are from meat-eating dinosaurs that appear to have been swimmers.

400 kilometers

0   400 miles

Do you want to join a dinosaur expedition? The Dinosaur Society (1-800-346-6366) has a list of all the organizations that sponsor digs where you can pay a fee to join in on the fun and adventure.

The top six most famous dinosaur quarries occur in Wyoming, Colorado, Montana, and Utah.

• FOSSIL KEY •

Late Cretaceous

Early Cretaceous

Late and Middle Jurassic

Early Jurassic

Triassic

More Dinosaur Stamps

Stamp collecting, or philately, is the most popular hobby in the world. It is practiced by all age groups in every country. Where else can you buy miniature pieces of international artwork for less than one dollar? Once a person starts collecting postage stamps, he or she can also trade them. Many postage stamps are found at stamp shows. It is also possible to "subscribe" to a postage stamp service that will automatically send new issues to your home. There is something very satisfying about finally hunting down and getting a "complete set" of any particular postage stamp you are collecting.

There are many different facets to stamp collecting. Most people collect all the postage stamps from their own country or from selected countries. One collecting specialty is known as FDC, or "first day covers." Some people collect only the cancellation marks! The fastest-growing area of stamp collecting is called *topicals*. In this hobby, people collect all the postage stamps based on a single theme, or topic. Prehistorics, fossils, and dinosaurs are a few such topics.

The first dinosaur postage stamp, issued by China in 1958, featured the prosauropod *Lufengosaurus*. Other dinosaur subjects began to appear, but the growth of this topic was slow. The United States issued its first dinosaur postage stamp in 1970, featuring part of the famous Rudolf Zallinger mural on display at the Peabody Museum of Natural History at Yale University. The next U.S. issue occurred in 1989 and featured three dinosaurs: "*Brontosaurus*," *Stegosaurus*, and *Allosaurus*. These were painted by paleoartist John Gurche. In 1992, the topic of dinosaurs exploded in anticipation of the movie *Jurassic Park* (Universal Studios, 1993). Within a few years, the number of dinosaur postage stamps had doubled worldwide. There are now two books just about collecting dinosaur stamps—one in English and the other in Japanese. A World Wide Web site listing dinosaur postage stamps will appear by 1998. The current release by famous artist/author James Gurney is the largest issue of dinosaur postage stamps at any one time by any country.

There are several "firsts" in this issue. This is the world premiere of the non-dinosaurs *Paleosaniwa*, a lizard; *Opisthias*, a sphenodontian; and *Goniopholis*, a crocodile. This is also the world premiere of the horned dinosaur *Einiosaurus*. ●

•BEST-SELLING POSTAGE STAMP•

Here's a little "DinoTrivia": Of all the dinosaurs featured in the postage stamps by James Gurney, which one has appeared on the most stamps? The answer is *Stegosaurus*—it has appeared on the postage stamps of 46 countries!

• DINOSAURS ARE INTERNATIONAL •

- *Dinosaur postage stamps have been issued by many countries, even countries that have found no dinosaur fossils! A list of all the dinosaur postage stamps that have been issued between 1842, the year the name "dinosaur" was coined, and 1992, the 150th anniversary, can be found in* The Complete Dinosaur, *Indiana University Press, 1997.*

- *Very few countries consult with dinosaur paleontologists about their postage stamps. This is because there are only about 80 professional dinosaur paleontologists in the world, and it is also cheaper and quicker for artists to work from old, popular books. Many postage stamps blatantly copy artwork from famous international paleontological artists such as Charles Knight, John Gurche, Rudolf Zallinger, and Zdenek Burian.*

- *The artwork on dinosaur postage stamps ranges from standard restorations to quite fanciful "artistic interpretations." Some of the most common mistakes are the use of outdated names such as "Brontosaurus," "Anatosaurus," and "Trachodon." The correct name for "Brontosaurus" is* Apatosaurus.

- *Do you know which stamps displayed on these two pages are not dinosaurs? The answer is Guyana and Nicaragua.*

Edmontonia

his armored dinosaur was named in 1928 by Charles Sternberg, of the famous Sternberg dynasty of field paleontologists. When this dinosaur was alive, most of western Canada and the northwest United States were the same place, paleontologically speaking.

Edmontonia, "near Edmonton," belongs to a subgroup of anky-losaurian dinosaurs known as nodosaurs. Although they do not have tail clubs, they do have very long and sharp shoulder spikes. These spikes are at the same height as the lower legs of the predatory dinosaurs such as *Daspletosaurus*. With a mass of more than a ton, *Edmontonia* threw its weight, using its shoulder spikes against the legs of any attacker. This may have been the first use of the "clipping penalty"! The armor in *Edmontonia* occurred in bands over the back that went from one side to the other. Each band was separated by skin; there-fore, these animals had flexible armor. The head also had armor fused onto the skull bones. This would be like having a football helmet permanently fused onto your skull!

The closest relatives of *Edmontonia* and the other nodosaurs are the family Polacanthidae, followed by the family Ankylosauridae with, of course, *Ankylosaurus*. *Edmontonia* averaged

• EDMONTONIA •
Near Edmonton

This armored herbivore lived in the Late Cretaceous period. The name is derived from where the first fossils were found: the Edmon-ton Formation in Alberta, Canada, now known as the Horseshoe Canyon Formation.

about 23 feet (7 meters) and weighed an astonishing 4 tons. It was an herbivore with a fairly narrow snout, which indicated that it was a selective eater, able to poke around for juicy new growth. The shoulder and flank spikes were capable of inflicting serious damage to any predator or competing male.

The model James Gurney used for this postage stamp was the specimen on display at the American Museum of Natural History in New York City, and also the flesh restoration (model) at the Royal Tyrrell Museum in Alberta, Canada. ●

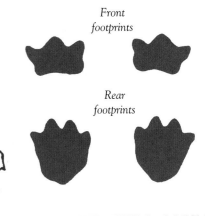

Front footprints

Rear footprints

• FOUR FEET, TWO SIZES •
Ankylosaur feet were wide and heavily muscled. The back feet were always larger because they supported more weight than the front feet.

• LIFE-SIZED •

This is a life-sized restoration at the Royal Tyrrell Museum in Alberta, Canada. It is comparable in size to a minivan vehicle.

Attachment ridges for jaw muscles

Eye

Nostril

• HELMET-HEAD •

Edmontonia's skull is composed of bone in two layers. The inner layer is the "regular" bone, and the outer layer is armor that has fused onto the skull.

Armor fused onto the skull bones

Eye

Beak

• NO SHOULDER PADS NEEDED •

These are several of *Edmontonia*'s shoulder spikes. They are roughly 15 inches long. If *Edmontonia* threw a shoulder block into the leg of a tyrannosaurid, it could break through muscles, tendons, and cartilage, crippling the attacker.

Einiosaurus

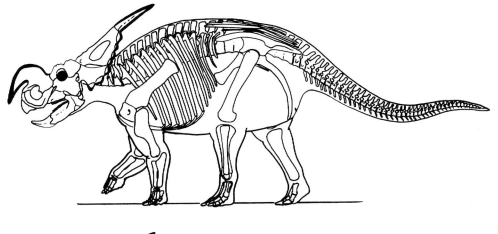

The ceratopsian, or horned, dinosaurs were one of the last major dinosaur groups to appear. Their most distinctive feature is the frill or shield at the back of the head. In 1995, Dr. Scott Sampson named this animal from skulls that were found in northern Montana in the Two Medicine Formation (Late Cretaceous). So far, Montana is the only known locality for this dinosaur.

Ceratopsians are famous for several reasons, one of which is the wide variety of frill shapes, including the ornamentations around the edges. It is most interesting to note that the entire frill is composed of the same two bones that form parts of human skulls: the squamosal and parietal bones. The spikes and other ornamentations are "new" bones that were not originally part of the standard set of skull bones. Each variety of spike shape and orientation, plus the different shapes of the nasal bones and horns, forms the basis for the recognition of species by paleontologists (and other ceratopsians).

There are many different kinds of horned dinosaurs, and they appear to have evolved rapidly, geologically speaking. There are two main groups of later ceratopsians, called chasmosaurs and centrosaurs. The most famous ornithischian, *Triceratops*, is one of the chasmosaurs. They are characterized by long horns over the eyes, a short nasal horn, complex folds of the nasal septum (a bone "inside" the nostril area), and few ornamentations around the edge of the frill. The centrosaurs are recognized by a large horn or roughened "boss" over the nose, short eye horns, a simple nasal septum, and many ornamentations around the frill.

The closest relatives of *Einiosaurus*, which means "buffalo lizard" in Blackfeet Indian lore, are the other centrosaurs, such as *Achelousaurus, Styracosaurus, Centrosaurus,* and *Pachyrhinosaurus.* Both the centrosaurs and chasmosaurs share a common ancestor in the famous *Protoceratops,* an early ceratopsian that was the size of a large dog. *Einiosaurus* was a plant eater with a narrow, hooked beak that could cut through fibrous plants. Groups of fossils found together suggest these ceratopsians traveled, ate, and defended themselves in herds.

The model for this postage stamp is the only known complete skull of *Einiosaurus,* now in the collection of the Museum of the Rockies in Bozeman, Montana. This is the world premiere of *Einiosaurus* on a postage stamp! ●

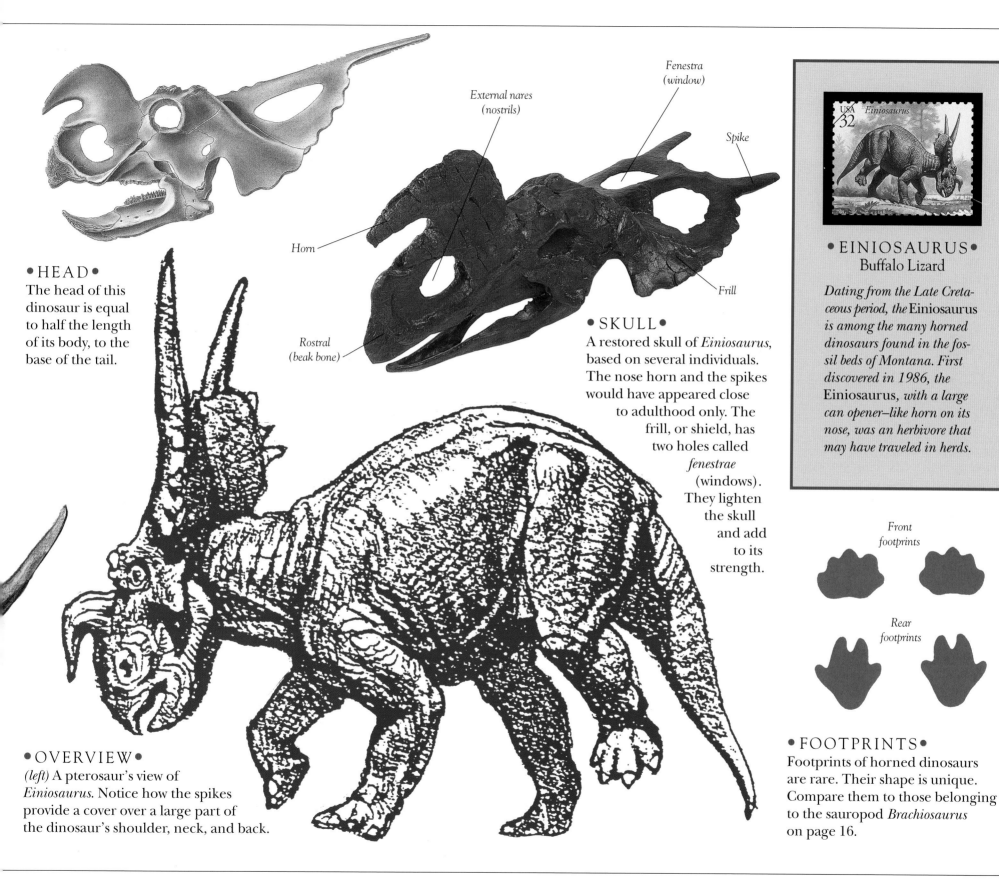

External nares (nostrils)

Fenestra (window)

Spike

Horn

Frill

Rostral (beak bone)

•HEAD•

The head of this dinosaur is equal to half the length of its body, to the base of the tail.

•SKULL•

A restored skull of *Einiosaurus*, based on several individuals. The nose horn and the spikes would have appeared close to adulthood only. The frill, or shield, has two holes called *fenestrae* (windows). They lighten the skull and add to its strength.

•EINIOSAURUS•
Buffalo Lizard

Dating from the Late Cretaceous period, the Einiosaurus *is among the many horned dinosaurs found in the fossil beds of Montana. First discovered in 1986, the* Einiosaurus, *with a large can opener–like horn on its nose, was an herbivore that may have traveled in herds.*

Front footprints

Rear footprints

•OVERVIEW•

(left) A pterosaur's view of *Einiosaurus*. Notice how the spikes provide a cover over a large part of the dinosaur's shoulder, neck, and back.

•FOOTPRINTS•

Footprints of horned dinosaurs are rare. Their shape is unique. Compare them to those belonging to the sauropod *Brachiosaurus* on page 16.

Daspletosaurus

T he mightiest carnivores of the Late Cretaceous of the American West were the tyrannosaurs, or "tyrant dinosaurs." Before *Tyrannosaurus rex* appeared, its somewhat smaller relative (and possible direct ancestor) *Daspletosaurus*, "frightful lizard," was the "king of dinosaurs." Named by Dale Russell in 1970, the first *Daspletosaurus* fossils were from the Judith River Group of Alberta, Canada. Since then, other fossils of this dinosaur have been found in Montana.

At 30 feet (9 meters) and over 3 tons, *Daspletosaurus* had a huge, powerfully built skull with very large teeth. Unlike the teeth of *Allosaurus* and other primitive theropod dinosaurs, those of tyrant dinosaurs were not knifelike. Tyrannosaur teeth were thick side to side, so they looked more like knife-edged bananas than like steak knives. The insides of the jaws of tyrant dinosaurs were very sturdy, indicating that they could twist off large chunks of flesh from their victims, whereas *Allosaurus* and other more primitive forms could only slice off pieces of meat.

Daspletosaurus, like all tyrant dinosaurs, had only two fingers on each hand. These fingers were too short to have been used to catch food, so they may have had some other function—perhaps for display, just as ostriches use their otherwise-useless wings in courtship. The legs of tyrant dinosaurs, though, were longer and more slender than those of other big predatory dinosaurs, and they ended in feet specially adapted to withstand the stresses of running. *Daspletosaurus* would have been faster than any of the big prey it was trying to catch, such as *Corythosaurus*. Like all advanced theropods, *Daspletosaurus* had a wishbone.

Daspletosaurus was a close relative, and possible ancestor, of the even larger *Tyrannosaurus*. Other relatives included *Gorgosaurus*, *Albertosaurus*, and other tyrant dinosaurs of Asia and western North America. Although it was long thought that the tyrannosaurs were the descendants of the allosaurs, recent studies demonstrate that the tyrant dinosaurs were actually more closely related to ostrich dinosaurs (such as *Ornithomimus*, page 42) and troodontids. Together,

the troodontids, ostrich dinosaurs, and tyrannosaurs form the Arctometatarsalia, one of the major subdivisions of the coelurosaurs (or birdlike theropods). Other groups of coelurosaurs include the dromaeosaurids (the "raptors" of *Jurassic Park* fame) and their close relatives, birds.

James Gurney's painting for this postage stamp is based on the skeleton of *Daspletosaurus* now on display at the Canadian Museum of Nature in Ottawa. ●

● DASPLETOSAURUS ●
Frightful Lizard

A close but smaller relative of Tyrannosaurus, Daspletosaurus *measured 30 feet long (9 meters) and weighed nearly 3½ tons. It was the top predator in its world.* Daspletosaurus *combined great strength and speed to be a deadly carnivore, despite arms no longer than a human's.*

● SWIFT AND SMART ●
With a long, narrow brain cavity showing highly developed sight, sound, and smell capacity, *Daspletosaurus* was built to hunt successfully.

● MR. BONES ●
The skeleton of *Daspletosaurus* shows the basic characteristics shared by all tyrannosaurs. Its skull and hind limbs were very powerful, but its arms were greatly reduced and had only two fingers each! The long tail counterbalanced the strong front end.

• FACE FORWARD •

The skull of *Daspletosaurus* (below) was 3 or more feet long, and lined with sharp, powerful teeth. The eyes of *Daspletosaurus* were directed forward to help focus on prey (although *Tyrannosaurus* had even better binocular vision than *Daspletosaurus*).

• A GIANT •

Although smaller than the later *Tyrannosaurus*, *Daspletosaurus* would dwarf any of today's land predators.

• CARNIVORE •

Daspletosaurus, with its long, sharp teeth, was clearly a meat eater. Like almost all modern carnivores, it got its food both by killing prey and by scavenging carcasses. Unable to lift prey to its mouth, this carnivore lowered its huge jaws to the ground to eat.

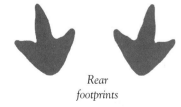

Rear footprints

Tyrannosaurs had short snouts

Eye socket

Teeth curved backward, better to hold prey

The lower jaw had a hinge in the back so it could open even wider, if necessary

The teeth were serrated on both front and back for easier cutting

• BIGFOOT! •

Footprints of *Daspletosaurus* and other tyrant dinosaurs are very rare. Like the tracks of other meat-eating dinosaurs, *Daspletosaurus* footprints show only the middle three toes touching the ground. The first toe (equivalent to our "big toe" or the backward toe on a chicken's foot) did not touch the ground, as seen in the sketch to the right.

Palaeosaniwa

While tyrannosaurids such as *Daspletosaurus* were the only large predators of the Late Cretaceous world, other creatures competed for prey with *Velociraptor*, *Dromaeosaurus*, and the other smaller meat-eating dinosaurs. Among such smaller carnivores were meat-eating lizards such as *Palaeosaniwa*, meaning "before *Saniwa*," a lizard from the early part of the age of mammals. Named by Charles Whitney Gilmore in 1928, the first described fossils of *Palaeosaniwa* were from an area near Steveville in Alberta, Canada. Although known only from fragmentary bones, *Palaeosaniwa*—or lizards very closely related to it—is found in most of the Late Cretaceous sedimentary rocks of the western part of North America, including Wyoming and Montana.

Like most true lizards, *Palaeosaniwa* had specialized jaw and skull joints that allowed the skull to flex and bend in different ways and to act as shock absorbers when the lizard ate live and large prey. From its teeth, we know that *Palaeosaniwa* was a meat eater, probably feeding on carrion, eggs, and smaller vertebrates, including baby dinosaurs. The details of its skull and vertebrae indicate that it was a close relative of the modern *Varanus*, or monitor lizard, of Africa, India, Southeast Asia, Australia, and the islands in between. *Palaeosaniwa* grew to be about as big as the modern Ora or Komodo dragon *(Varanus komodoensis)*, perhaps 10–12 feet (3–3.5 meters) long and 330 pounds (150 kilograms). Although not as sophisticated a predator as the smaller meat-eating dinosaurs, *Palaeosaniwa* could probably kill smaller dinosaurs just as the Ora kills pigs, dogs, and deer today.

Palaeosaniwa and *Varanus* are just two types of the large assemblage of varanoid lizards. Some varanoids, such as the modern Gila monster (*Heloderma*) of southwestern North America and the larger Cretaceous *Estesia* of Mongolia, have poisonous fangs. *Palaeosaniwa* and *Varanus* show the typical lizard shape: a long snout with a forked tongue, a long body with four legs ending in five claws each, and a long, slender tail. However, some Cretaceous varanoids evolved into a very different body shape, like the 10-to-46-foot (3-to-14-meter) mosasauroids, which were swimming forms with flippers instead of feet. Another closely related branch of the varanoids evolved without any legs. This specialized group of varanoid lizards is still living today; we call them "snakes."

This is the first time *Palaeosaniwa* has been shown on a postage stamp! ●

• PALAEOSANIWA •
Note how lizards have outwardly flexed elbows and knees, unlike dinosaurs.

• PALAEOSANIWA •
Before Saniwa

Related to the modern monitor lizards, of which Indonesia's Komodo dragon is the largest living example, these creatures survived the mass extinction of the dinosaurs.

Palaeosaniwa
USA 32

• SKULL OF ESTESIA •

A relative of *Palaeosaniwa*, *Estesia* was a carnivorous lizard from the Late Cretaceous of Mongolia. Like today's Gila monster, it was poisonous.

Nose

Eye

Teeth row

Joint in jaw so the front half could move separately from the back half

• AN EXTINCT MONITOR •

Although we know little of the skeleton of *Palaeosaniwa*, the parts that are known are very similar to those of today's monitor lizards *(right)*. Using these modern examples, paleontologists think that *Paleosaniwa* looks much like the sketch shown here.

• MODERN MONITOR LIZARDS •

The monitor lizards (species of *Varanus*) are commonly found in several parts of the world today. Among these are the Goanna *(Varanus gouldii)* of Australia *(top)*, the Ora or Komodo dragon *(Varanus komodoensis)* of Indonesia *(middle)*, and the Nile monitor *(Varanus niloticus)* of Africa *(bottom)*.

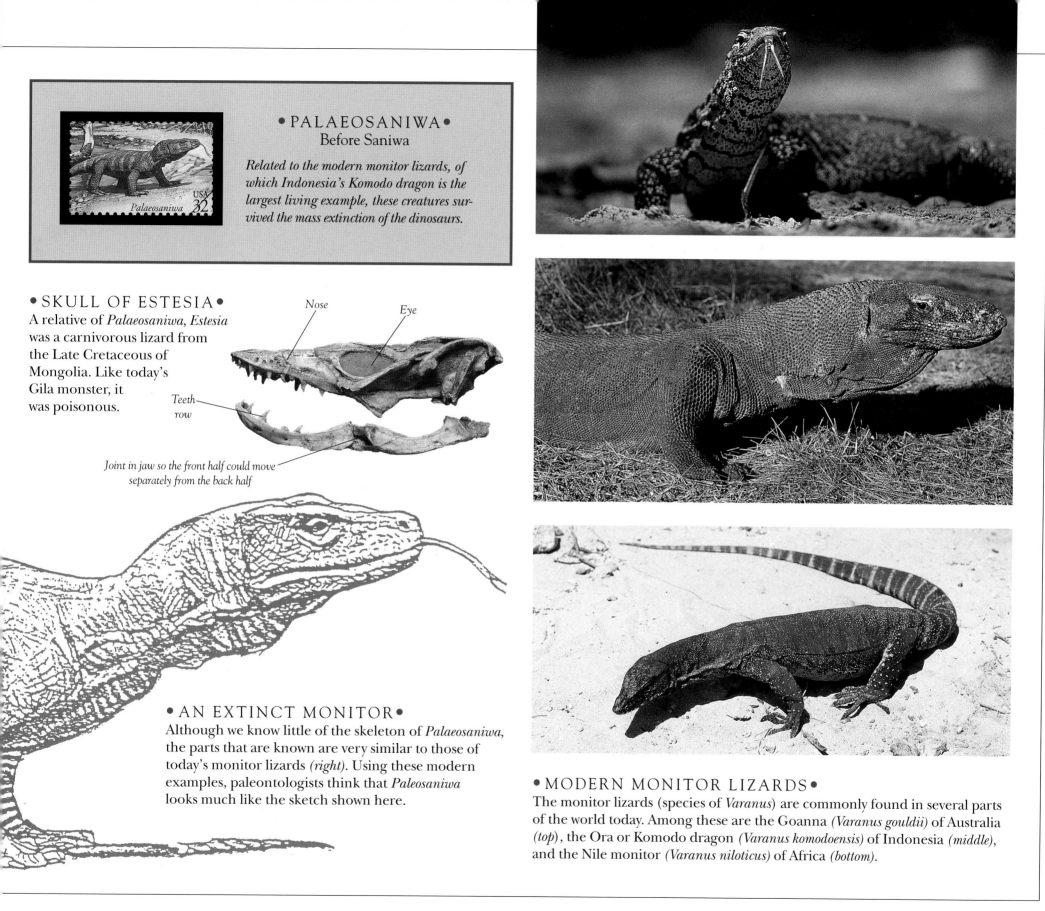

Corythosaurus

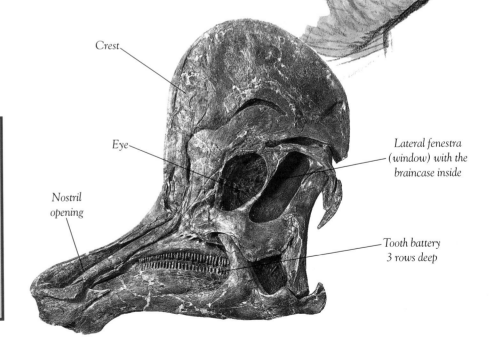

alled "Corinthian helmet lizard," this Late Cretaceous duck-billed dinosaur was named in 1914 by the greatest field paleontologist of all time: Barnum Brown of the American Museum of Natural History in New York City. The name refers to the shape of its crest, which looks very much like the helmet of the hoplite warriors in ancient Greece. *Corythosaurus* has been found in Canada and in Montana.

This is one of the most elegant herbivorous dinosaurs. Its crest is composed of the premaxilla—upper lip bone—and the nasal bones. Inside are several hollow chambers that serve many functions. In addition to increasing the sense of smell, the air passage that runs through the crest may have been used for making "infrasound." These are sounds of very low frequencies that can travel for many miles. Elephants use this method to communicate the presence of water. By blowing air through their noses at different frequencies, duckbill dinosaurs may have sounded like the very first woodwind and reed instruments.

Duckbill dinosaurs had ever-growing and self-sharpening teeth that were 3 ranks deep and up to 60 rows long (in *Anatotitan*). Replacement teeth came up from below, like an escalator. They were used for grinding up plant food before it was swallowed. This was unique for dinosaurs. Most other groups did not chew food like humans—they just swallowed it whole.

Duckbill dinosaurs and other ornithopods were not built for speed like the theropods, but they were more maneuverable. If they traveled in vast herds, as most paleontologists believe, then it was their best form of protection.

The closest relatives of the duckbills are the iguanodonts, like *Iguanodon* and *Ouranosaurus*, followed by the camptosaurs.

The model for this postage stamp is the fantastic mummified *Corythosaurus* on display at the American Museum of Natural History in New York. ●

● THE SKULL ●
This skull from the American Museum of Natural History is one of the most complete dinosaurs skulls known. Notice that the teeth are only in the mid-part of the jaw. There are no teeth up front.

● A COMBINATION OF A HORSE AND A MOOSE ●
Hadrosaurs were all herbivores with an increased sense of smell and a unique skull "ornament." *Corythosaurus* forelimbs ended in flat, fingerlike hooves, which indicates that the dinosaur probably walked on four legs occasionally.

● CORYTHOSAURUS ●
Corinthian Helmet Lizard

Corythosaurus was an herbivore of the Late Cretaceous period with a duck bill and a rough, pebble-textured skin. The closest relatives of Corythosaurus *were* Lambeosaurus *and* Hypacrosaurus.

Crest

Eye

Nostril opening

Lateral fenestra (window) with the braincase inside

Tooth battery 3 rows deep

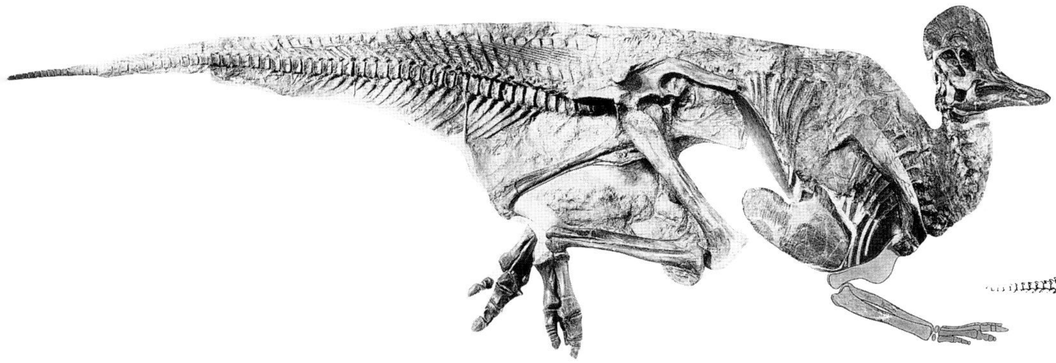

This is a skeletal restoration from the original scientific paper that described this specimen. This particular figure shows the dinosaur in its "death pose," the way it was found in the field. It is designed to show scientists key features that were preserved.

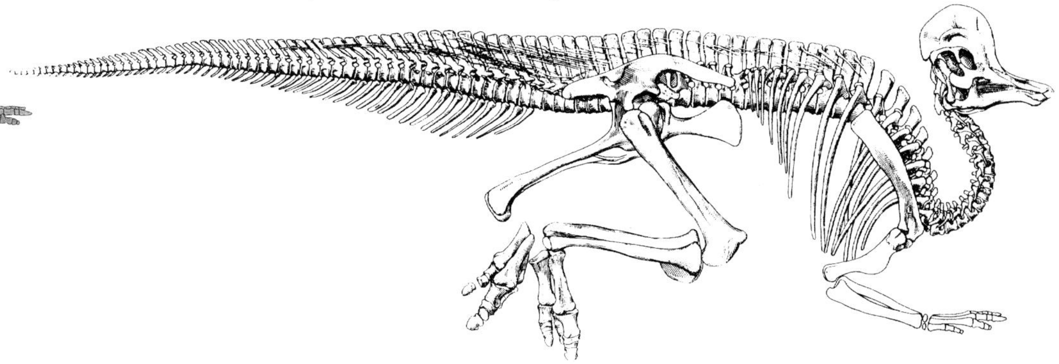

• NOW YOU SEE HIM... •

This is one of the skeletons that showed how the duckbill's tail was erect and did not drag on the ground. Skin impressions, which were also found from this specimen, show a bumpy kind of scales.

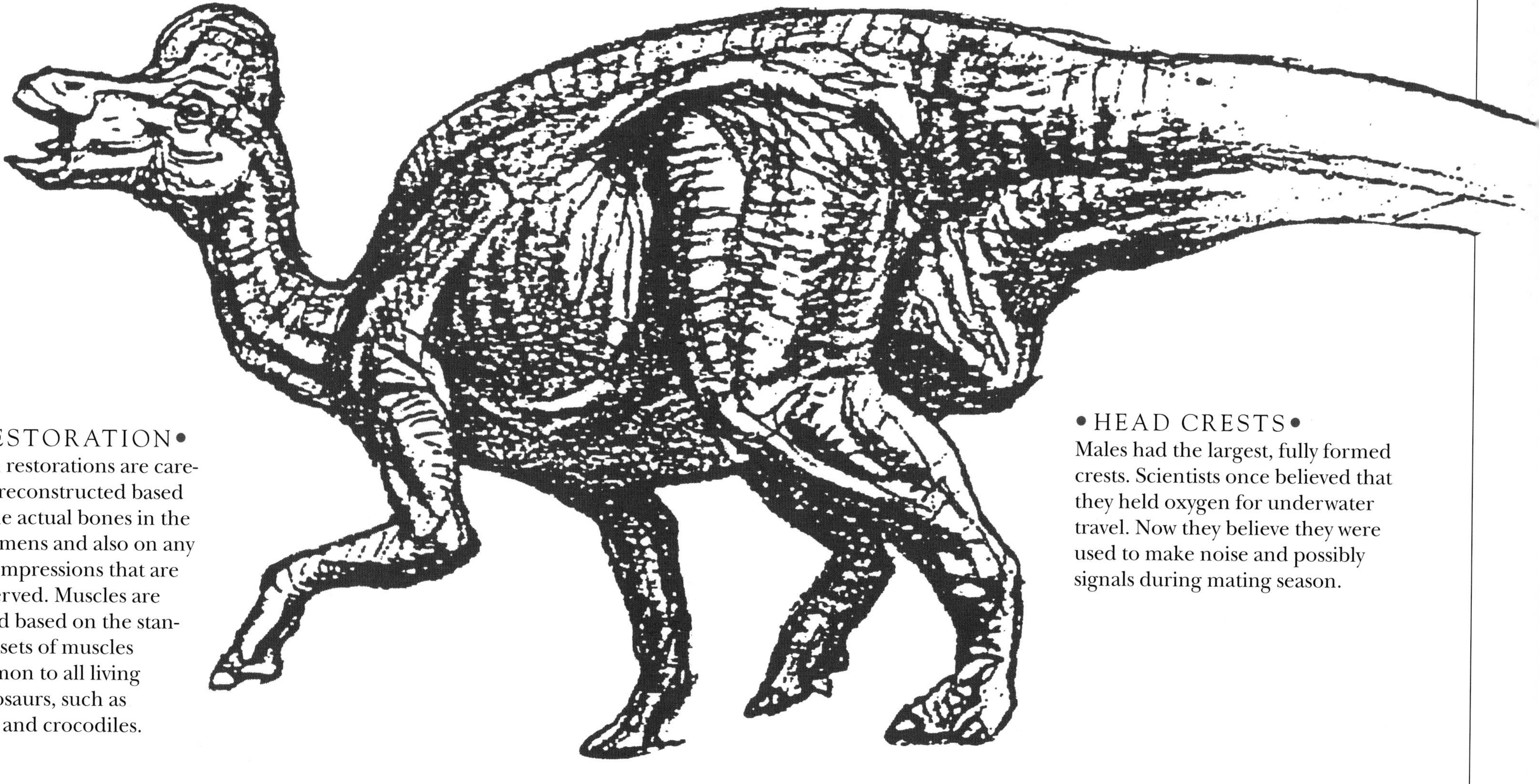

• RESTORATION •

Flesh restorations are carefully reconstructed based on the actual bones in the specimens and also on any skin impressions that are preserved. Muscles are added based on the standard sets of muscles common to all living archosaurs, such as birds and crocodiles.

• HEAD CRESTS •

Males had the largest, fully formed crests. Scientists once believed that they held oxygen for underwater travel. Now they believe they were used to make noise and possibly signals during mating season.

Ornithomimus

O thniel Charles Marsh named this dinosaur in 1890, when only the foot, the shin, and the hand had been discovered in Jefferson County, Colorado. Complete skeletons found after the turn of the century showed that the name was even more accurate than Marsh could have guessed! Over the years, fossils of *Ornithomimus*, "bird mimic," have been found in Utah, Montana, and Alberta.

Ornithomimus, a fairly typical ostrich dinosaur, had a toothless beak; a long, slender neck; arms ending in specialized hooking and clamping hands; very long legs; and a long tail. The ostrich dinosaur looked very much like an ostrich with arms instead of wings! At 5 feet (1.5 meters) high at the hips and 365 pounds (165 kilograms), it was about as big as an ostrich as well.

The toothless beak of the ostrich dinosaur suggests that it, like the modern ostrich, was an omnivore. It may have eaten small animals, leaves, fruit, eggs, worms, or anything else it could peck or grab. Unlike most theropod dinosaurs, it did not have hands tipped with talons. Instead, its hands could form a hook to grab onto branches, perhaps to bring leaves and fruit closer to its beak.

Ornithomimus legs were very long and slender, and their feet, like those of tyrant dinosaurs, had specialized shock-absorbing structures. Most paleontologists agree that ostrich dinosaurs were the fastest dinosaurs. *Ornithomimus* had good reason to be a fast runner, since *Daspletosaurus*, and later *Tyrannosaurus*, stalked the same woods and fields.

Ornithomimus is one of the best-known ostrich dinosaurs. Other ostrich dinosaurs, such as *Struthiomimus*, *Dromiceiomimus*, and *Gallimimus*, which are known only from fossils, are found in the Late Cretaceous of Asia and western North America. *Deinocheirus* is known only from fossils of its enormous arms. More primitive ostrich dinosaurs are found in the Early Cretaceous. The best known is Spanish *Pelecanimimus*, which was not toothless but instead had more than 220 teeth. The closest relatives of the ostrich dinosaurs were the brainy troodontids, and these two groups together form a group called Bullatosauria.

The best skeletons of *Ornithomimus*, which form the basis of James Gurney's paintings, are on display at the Royal Ontario Museum in Toronto, Canada, and the American Museum of Natural History in New York City. ●

Rear footprints

• FOOTPRINTS •

Ornithomimus ran on the three middle toes of the foot, just like birds do today. However, unlike birds, ostrich dinosaurs lost the first toe, the toe that sticks back on the foot of a chicken.

• ORNITHOMIMUS •

Built for speed, *Ornithomimus* was probably among the fastest dinosaurs. It had long, slender hind limbs with special adaptations for absorbing the shock of running. At full speed, it may have tucked its arms into the body to reduce wind resistance.

• ORNITHOMIMUS •
Bird Mimic

At approximately 5 feet and 363 pounds, the size of a large ostrich, Ornithomimus was probably almost as fast. With its large brain, it was probably among the smartest dinosaurs, too.

• THE HEAD •

The head of *Ornithomimus* is one of its most birdlike features. Instead of teeth, it had toothless jaws with a horny "beak," just like birds or turtles today. *Ornithomimus* had very large eyes and one of the largest brains of all the dinosaurs relative to its body size.

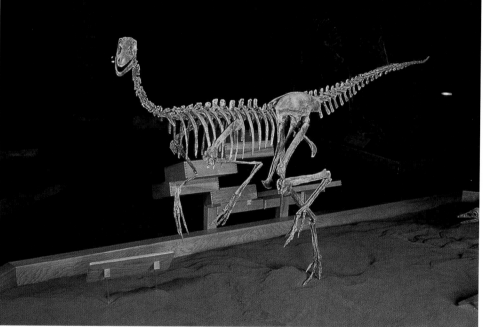

• LUNCH! •

Most paleontologists think that *Ornithomimus* was an omnivore, eating both meat, like the small mammal to the left, and plants.

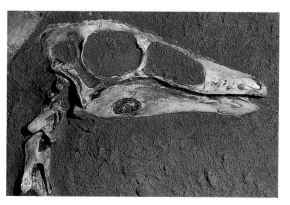

• SKELETON •

Skeletons of *Ornithomimus* and other ostrich dinosaurs show that they were swift and lightly built. Their long arms were probably used to hold food, either plants or animals.

Parasaurolophus

his duckbill dinosaur is one of the most famous dinosaurs and the most frequently pictured duckbill. *Parasaurolophus*, "like *Saurolophus*," was also featured in the movie *The Lost World* (Universal Studios, 1997). William Parks named this dinosaur in 1922, based on a specimen from Dinosaur Provincial Park in Alberta, Canada. Other specimens have been found in Montana and, especially, in New Mexico. The name refers to the fact that the crest of this dinosaur looks like that of *Saurolophus*, which had a short, solid crest. In *Parasaurolophus*, could be over 4 feet long, and it was hollow.

The crest of *Parasaurolophus* is unique in the animal world and came in a wide variety of sizes. One specimen had a short crest and a large body. Another had a longer crest and a smaller body. Could these be female and male? In the mid-1990s, a new specimen was found in New Mexico by paleontologists Tom Williamson and Robert Sullivan. This new specimen had a crest that was much more complex than those of previously known specimens. Up until this time, it was assumed that there were four main tubes, or chambers, that ran inside the crest. The New Mexico specimen had six main chambers. Could this be the result of variations within a population, or possible age differences? Could this be a new species? For now, the sample size is too small for paleontologists to adequately test this idea, because this dinosaur is one of the rarest of all the ornithopods.

Duckbills are also famous for the sounds that the nasal complex might have generated. From fossils, we know that cavities in these crests were connected to the nasal passages and windpipe. Some scientists imagine that the non-crested group could generate sounds much like reed instruments in today's orchestras. The crested group would be like the woodwinds. Each species could make its own unique sounds that would reverberate through the Mesozoic forests.

The closest relatives of the crested duckbills like

•PARASAUROLOPHUS•
Like Saurolophus

With a crest over 4 feet long, this duckbill had the longest nasal chambers of any dinosaur. It is thought to have amplified this creature's honking sounds.

Parasaurolophus are *Corythosaurus* and *Lambeosaurus*. The next closest group are the non-crested duckbills, such as *Anatotitan, Kritosaurus, Maiasaura,* and *Saurolophus*. Duckbills as a group are related to the iguanodonts.

The model for this postage stamp was the mounted skeleton on display in the Royal Ontario Museum in Toronto, Canada. •

•CRESTED•
Crests may have been as brightly colored as a toucan's bill.

•A TALL DRINK•
Dinosaurs did not need as much water as mammals. They also got water from the plants that they ate.

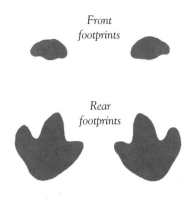

Front footprints

Rear footprints

• FROM HEAD TO TOE •

The beaks of duckbills had a horned sheath that covered the mouth. It was very sharp and was used to cut up plant food. Their teeth began farther back in the jaw. The front prints of duckbills were quite small compared to hind prints. The hind prints were made by three fingers inside a mitten of skin. Because the stride of the front limbs was shorter than the stride of the hind limbs, hadrosaurs ran on just the hind legs. The front limbs could not keep up the same pace as the hind limbs at full speed.

•AS IT MAY HAVE LIVED•

This is the exhibit of *Parasaurolophus* in the Royal Ontario Museum in Toronto, Canada. The skeleton is about 6 feet high. Scientists believe these dinosaurs traveled in herds, following seasonal vegetation growth. Perhaps their colorful crests helped them to recognize each other.

• X-RAY VISION! •

Note how flexible the neck appears to be, and the powerful hind legs that allowed it to stand to reach higher vegetation. Only *Parasaurolophus* had the distinctive long, hollow crest. Females may have had smaller crests. The bones that formed the crest are the same ones that formed the upper "lip" of the mouth. In no other animal did the "lip" go behind the skull.

•FAMILY TREE•

Parasaurolophus was a hadrosaur ("duckbill") in the lambeosaurid family. They were all plant eaters.

About The Artist

WHEN JAMES GURNEY was in grade school, it was hard to find books on dinosaurs. "None of my friends talked about them," he said. "And they definitely weren't cool at my school." But one day his parents took him to a museum near where he grew up in Palo Alto, California. There he saw a mounted skeleton of an *Allosaurus.* "At first I thought dinosaurs *were* skeletons, because every time you saw a dinosaur in a museum, it was always just bones." He daydreamed that this skeleton would come to life after the janitors closed up the museum for the night. "I pictured it stepping over the railing and stalking through the corridors before it returned at daybreak. To me, that's the reason dinosaurs are so fascinating. They just won't stay dead."

Gurney's daydreams took him beyond dinosaurs into archaeology and lost civilizations. Outside his bedroom door was a shelf of *National Geographic* magazines dating back to 1915. He would read late into the night about pilots in biplanes flying over uncharted Inca and Maya ruins. After school, he would dig "excavation pits" in his suburban backyard, hoping to find arrowheads or maybe even a lost temple. "My friends' mothers quit letting their kids play at my house because they always came home covered with dirt," he said. Even though he didn't find much of what he imagined, he made up for it by sculpting it out of clay or drawing it on paper.

By the time he went to college at the University of California at Berkeley, he sought out the professors who loved archaeology and paleontology. They were kind enough to let him explore the museum collections. One of his first jobs was making careful drawings of Egyptian scarab carvings for a scientist's publication. After participating on a real archaeological dig with the legendary James Deetz, he decided to major in anthropology.

He then pursued his interest in drawing and painting by studying at the Art Center College of Design in Pasadena. He sketched outdoors at every opportunity. A cross-country trip on railroad boxcars led to a book that he cowrote and illustrated with his friend Thomas Kinkade, called *The Artist's Guide to Sketching* (Watson-Guptil, 1982). He worked for a time in the movie industry, painting background scenes of jungles and volcanoes for the film *Fire and Ice,* (Bakshi/Frazetta, 1983).

Gurney's big break came when *National Geographic* invited him to illustrate an article on the explorer Alexander Humboldt, an assignment that was soon followed by many others, including ones on the civilizations of Kush in Nubia, Etruscans in Italy, and Moche in Peru. Each assignment was a stimulating chance to work with experts to picture in the mind's eye a world that could never be photographed. Whenever he would get to know the Indiana Jones–

Artist James Gurney in his studio, surrounded by his props and models.

type archaeologists like Rick Bronson or Tim Kendall, he would discover that each of them shared his secret dream of discovering a lost city. Gurney reasoned that he could always paint such a city. In his spare time, he created *Waterfall City* and *Dinosaur Parade*, two paintings that led to the idea of an island populated by dinosaurs and people. During the five years it has taken Gurney to write and illustrate his two books, *Dinotopia: A Land Apart from Time* and *Dinotopia: The World Beneath*, he has immersed himself in every detail of the island, from maps to mechanics to metaphysics. *Dinotopia* has gone on to win many awards and is available in more than 30 countries worldwide. It was featured on the cover of *Smithsonian* magazine in September of 1995.

Dinotopia revived Gurney's boyhood interest in dinosaurs, and he has enjoyed learning about the new science of dynamic dinosaurs from the experts themselves, including the authors of this book—Brett-Surman, Holtz, and Jack Horner, who wrote the introduction. All three contributed to making *Dinotopia* as accurate as possible.

Gurney lives in the Hudson Valley of New York with his wife, two sons, and a calico cat, which crouches in his studio amid his model dinosaurs, seeming to wonder, "Why weren't there calico dinosaurs?" ●

About The Writers

MICHAEL K. BRETT-SURMAN grew up in Larchmont, New York. He was one of the many children who was permanently affected by seeing the skeleton of *Tyrannosaurus rex* at the American Museum of Natural History in New York City. He attended the University of Colorado, Boulder, initially as business major. He switched to anthropology to continue his interest in the geologic past.

One of the professors who influenced him most was paleontologist H. E. Koerner (who, incidentally, bore a passing resemblance to famous paleontologist E. D. Cope). With the increasing belief that most anthropologists were "graduates of the Twilight Zone," Brett-Surman moved further back in time to the Mesozoic era. Upon entering graduate school at the University of California, Berkeley, he specialized in dinosaurs. At this time, there were only 20 dinosaur specialists in the world, as compared to the 80 or so now. After obtaining a master's degree on the anatomy of hadrosaurian (duckbill) dinosaurs, he transferred to the Johns Hopkins University to continue his studies. This move resulted in a once-in-a-lifetime accident. While doing research at the Smithsonian Institution, he asked the curator, Dr. Nicholas Hotton, if

there were any "spare jobs" in the Paleobiology Department. An opening had appeared that same week. Without hesitation, Brett-Surman took the job and began a career that started in 1979. In 1988, he finished his Ph.D. by going to school part-time at George Washington University. He has named three new dinosaurs for science: *Secernosaurus*, *Gilmorosaurus* and *Anatotitan*.

Michael Brett-Surman is the coeditor of *The Complete Dinosaur*, Indiana University Press, 1997. He resides in Northern Virginia, with his wife and three black cats.

THOMAS R. HOLTZ, JR., was born in Los Angeles, California, but lived outside of Houston, Texas, until he was ten. After being convinced by his parents that he could not, under any circumstances, grow up to be a dinosaur, he decided to do the next best thing—study them! His first encounter with real dinosaur skeletons was a trip to Dinosaur National Monument and other Western museums when he was seven (and already convinced that a life dedicated to vertebrate paleontology was his goal).

Holtz attended the Johns Hopkins University. His studies with Steve Stanley made him appreciate that there was more to paleontology than dinosaurs. Nonetheless, he was never convinced that there were more interesting things in paleontology than dinosaurs, and so, after graduation, he entered the Department of Geology and Geophysics at Yale University, right next door to the Peabody Museum of Natural History, O. C. Marsh's old haunt. At Yale, he studied under Professor John Ostrom, who discovered the "raptor" *Deinonychus* and who was the key figure in discovering the dinosaurian origin of birds. Holtz earned his Ph.D. in 1992 by studying the functional adaptations of tyrannosaur feet and revising the evolutionary history of theropods.

After earning his doctorate, Holtz worked in a laboratory of the climate change program of the U.S. Geological Survey at Reston, Virginia. At that time, the Department of Geology at the University of Maryland, College Park, was searching for someone to teach a course on dinosaurs. He joined the department full-time in 1995, and he continues to teach two dinosaur courses, as well as courses on invertebrate paleontology and historical and environmental geology. He currently lives in Maryland with his wife and two cats. ●

Shown at the field camp of the Smithsonian's Wyoming Dinosaur Expedition in 1994 are Dr. Thomas R. Holtz, Jr. (left), portraying a maniraptoran hand; Charles Martin (center), displaying a tyrannosaurid hand; and M. K. Brett-Surman, Ph.D. (right), demonstrating a ceratosaur hand. The smiles, however, are distinctively human.

Credits

Inquiries should be addressed to The Greenwich Workshop, Inc., P.O. Box 875, Shelton, Connecticut 06484-0875.

For information about the art of James Gurney, please write to The Greenwich Workshop, Inc., at the address above, or call us at 1-800-243-4246.

Library of Congress Cataloging-in-Publication Data:
Brett-Surman, M.K., 1950–   James Gurney : the world of
    dinosaurs / Michael Brett-Surman, Thomas R. Holtz, Jr. ;
    introduction by Jack Horner.
p. cm.   ISBN 0-86713-046-6 (alk. paper)

Summary: Text and illustrations, based on James Gurney's art
    commissioned for the Postal Service dinosaur stamp series,
    introduce thirteen dinosaurs and three other creatures found
    in North America during the Jurassic and Cretaceous periods.
1. Dinosaurs—United States—Juvenile literature.   2. Gurney,
    James, 1958– —Juvenile literature.   3. Dinosaurs on postage
    stamps—Juvenile literature.   [1. Dinosaurs.   2. Dinosaurs
    on postage stamps.   3. Postage stamps.] I. Gurney,
    James, 1958– II. Holtz, Thomas R., 1965– . III. Title.
QE862.D5B675   1998   567.9'0973—dc21
97-48261   CIP   AC

A GREENWICH WORKSHOP PRESS BOOK

Postage stamp design TM & ©1998 USPS. All rights reserved. Produced under license by The Greenwich Workshop, Inc. All artwork is ©1997 by James Gurney, except as noted below.

• • •

ACKNOWLEDGMENTS

The Greenwich Workshop Press wishes to thank the following individuals and organizations for their permission to use the artwork noted:

P. 3, *top left,* #46528, courtesy Department of Library Services, the American Museum of Natural History. P. 10, drawings of *Ceratosaurus* ©The Bettmann Archive. P. 11, *top left, Ceratosaurus* skeleton, courtesy of the Smithsonian Institution; skeletal drawing of *Ceratosaurus* ©Greg Paul. P. 12, *Camptosaurus* skeleton model ©Royal Ontario Museum. P. 13, *left, Camptosaurus* with *Allosaurus* skeletal exhibit ©Natural History Museum of Los Angeles County; *right, Camptosaurus* painting, Salamander Picture Library. P. 15, *top left,* juvenile *Camarasaurus* skeleton ©Carnegie Museum of Natural History; *top right, Camarasaurus* skull photo, courtesy of the Smithsonian Institution. P. 16, *left, Brachiosaurus* skeletal drawing ©Greg Paul. P. 17, *left, Brachiosaurus* skull ©1997 Kenneth Carpenter; *right, Brachiosaurus* skeleton reconstruction ©1997 Louis Psihoyos/Matrix. P. 18, *top, Goniopholis* skull, from the collection of the American Museum of Natural History, courtesy of Royal Tyrrell Museum/Alberta Community Development. P. 19, *top left,* Nile crocodile feeding ©Fritz Polking/Peter Arnold, Inc.; *top right,* crocodilian skull ©Luiz C. Marigo/Peter Arnold, Inc. P. 21, *top left, Stegosaurus* spike, ©Museum of the Rockies; *top right, Stegosaurus* tail plate, ©Museum of the Rockies; *bottom right, Stegosaurus* specimen, courtesy of the Smithsonian Institution. P. 23, *top, Allosaurus* skeleton, ©Museum of the Rockies; *bottom right, Allosaurus* skeletal drawing ©Greg Paul. P. 25, *top left,* tuatara ©John Cancalosi/Peter Arnold, Inc.; *center and bottom right, Opisthias* skull and reconstruction drawings ©Virginia Museum of Natural History. P. 28, #132103, courtesy Department of Library Services, the American Museum of Natural History. P. 33, *top left, Edmontonia* ©Royal Tyrrell Museum/Alberta Community Development; *center right, Edmontonia* skull

reconstruction, negative 16, from the collection of the American Museum of Natural History, courtesy of Dr. Walter Coombs; *bottom right, Edmontonia* dermal spines, courtesy of the Smithsonian Institution. P. 34, *top and center right, Einio-saurus* skeletal and reconstruction drawings ©Tracy Ford. P. 35, *top left, Einiosaurus* skull drawing ©1995 Kris Ellingsen; *center, Einiosaurus* skull, ©Museum of the Rockies. P. 36, *Daspletosaurus* skeletal drawing ©Greg Paul. P. 37, *center, Daspletosaurus* skull, ©Museum of the Rockies. P. 39, *left, Palaeosaniwa* skull, #2A23710, courtesy Department of Library Services, the American Museum of Natural History; *top right,* Goanna ©Fred Bruemmer/Peter Arnold, Inc.; *center,* Komodo dragon ©Fred Bruemmer/Peter Arnold, Inc.; *bottom,* Nile monitor ©BIOS/Peter Arnold, Inc. P. 40, *bottom,*

Corythosaurus, #35876, courtesy Department of Library Services, the American Museum of Natural History. P. 41, *top left, Corytho-saurus,* #36211, courtesy Department of Library Services, the American Museum of Natural History; *top right, Corythosaurus* skeletal drawing, #36213, courtesy Department of Library Services, the American Museum of Natural History. P. 43, *top left, Ornitho-mimus* head drawing ©Robert Walters; *center right, Ornithomimus* skeleton ©Royal Tyrrell Museum/Alberta Community Development; *bottom right, Struthiomimus* skull ©Royal Tyrrell Museum/ Alberta Community Development. P. 44, *left, Parasaurolophus* head ©1992 James Gurney, reprinted, by permission, from *Dinotopia* (1992, Turner Publishing, Inc.). P. 45, *left, Parasaurolophus* model ©Royal Ontario Museum; *bottom, Parasaurolophus* skeletal drawing ©Greg Paul. P. 46, James Gurney photo by Jeanette Gurney. P. 47, photo ©1995 Kenneth D. Gadow.

• • •

The Greenwich Workshop wishes to acknowledge the contributions of the following in the research of this publication:

Donna Braginetz; Brent Breithaupt, museum director of the University of Wyoming Geological Museum; Brooks Britt, Dinosaur Valley Museum; Thomas Carr; Chantal Dessault, archivist of the Canada Museum of Nature in Ottawa; Dr. Peter Dodson, professor of veterinary anatomy and geology, University of Pennsylvania, School of Veterinary Medicine; Bill Parsons; Edward R. Ricciuti; Dale Russell, Department of Marine, Earth and Atmospheric Science, North Carolina State University; Dr. Scott Sampson, Department of Anatomy, New York College of Osteopathic Medicine; Carol M. Spawn, archivist, Philadelphia Academy of Natural Science; Susan Swan, publishing officer, Canada Museum of Nature in Ottawa; and Dave Thomas.

• • •

You can order *The World of Dinosaurs* postage stamps by calling 1-800-STAMP-24.

• • •

Book design by Judy Turziano
Manufactured in Singapore by CS Graphics
First Printing 1998
98 99 00 9 8 7 6 5 4 3 2 1

A Scene in Montana,

Edmontonia, Einiosaurus, Daspletosaurus, Palaeosan

150 Million Years Ago

...aurus, Goniopholis, Stegosaurus, Allosaurus, Opisthias

A Scene in Colorado,

Ceratosaurus, Camptosaurus, Camarasaurus, Brachios

75 Million Years Ago

iwa, Corythosaurus, Ornithomimus, Parasaurolophus

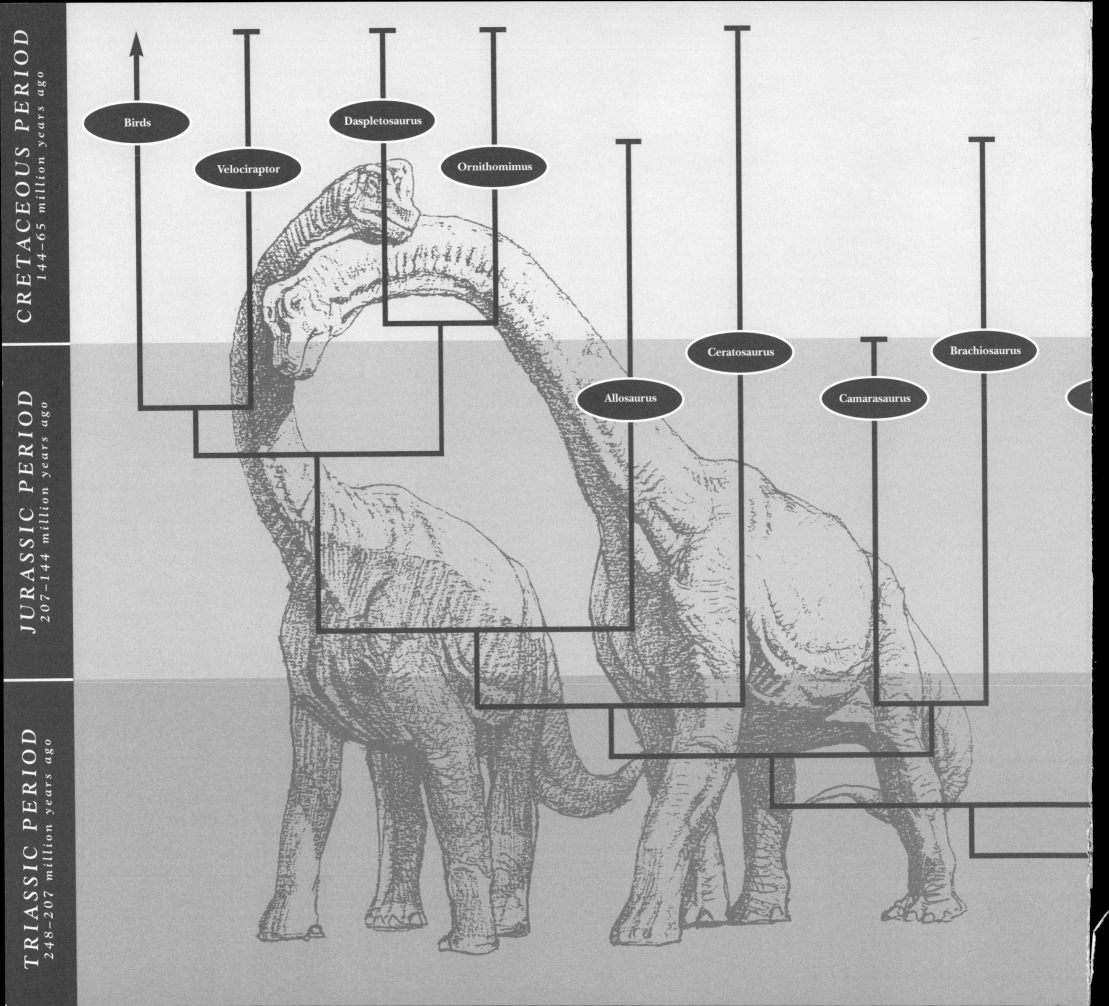

CRETACEOUS PERIOD
144–65 million years ago

JURASSIC PERIOD
207–144 million years ago

TRIASSIC PERIOD
248–207 million years ago

Birds

Velociraptor

Daspletosaurus

Ornithomimus

Allosaurus

Ceratosaurus

Camarasaurus

Brachiosaurus